SCM STUDYGUIDE TO PASTORAL THEOLOGY

Also available

SCM Studyguide to Theological Reflection
SCM Studyguide to Christian Ethics
SCM Studyguide to Old Testament
SCM Studyguide to The Books of the New Testament
SCM Studyguide to New Testament Interpretation
SCM Studyguide to Biblical Hermeneutics
SCM Studyguide to Christian Doctrine
SCM Studyguide to Science and Religion
SCM Studyguide to Early Christian Doctrine and the Creeds
SCM Studyguide to Church History
SCM Studyguide to The Sacraments
SCM Studyguide to Anglicanism
SCM Studyguide to The Psalms
SCM Studyguide to Preaching
SCM Studyguide to Practical Skills for Ministry
SCM Studyguide to Christian Spirituality
SCM Studyguide to Liturgy

SCM STUDYGUIDE TO PASTORAL THEOLOGY

Margaret Whipp

scm press

© Margaret Whipp 2013

Published in 2013 by SCM Press
Editorial office
3rd Floor
Invicta House
108-114 Golden Lane,
London EC1Y 0TG

SCM Press is an imprint of Hymns Ancient & Modern Ltd
(a registered charity)
13A Hellesdon Park Road
Norwich NR6 5DR, UK

www.scmpress.co.uk

All rights reserved. No part of this publication may be
reproduced, stored in a retrieval system, or transmitted,
in any form or by any means, electronic, mechanical,
photocopying or otherwise, without the prior permission of
the publisher, SCM Press.

The Author has asserted her right under the Copyright, Designs
and Patents Act, 1988, to be identified as the Author of this Work

British Library Cataloguing in Publication data

A catalogue record for this book is available
from the British Library

978-0-334-04550-2
Kindle edition 978-0-334-04551-9

Typeset by Regent Typesetting, London
Printed and bound by
CPI Group (UK) Ltd, Croydon

Contents

List of Figures	vi
1 The Humble Pastor – Imagining Pastoral Care	1

Part 1 Life in all its Fullness: The Call to be Human

2 Being Human – Life, Love and Longings	17
3 Faithful Change – Growth, Transition and Maturity	32
4 All Desires Known – Sexuality and the Call of Love	51
5 The Fragility of Life – Attachment, Trauma and Loss	68
6 Growing Together – Religion, Relationships and Ritual	87

Part 2 For Their Sakes: The Call to Care

7 Tend my Flock – The Story of Pastoral Care	105
8 The Art of Pastoral Conversation – Listening, Love and Language	126
9 Boundaries and Power – The Limits of Pastoral Care	141
10 Serpents and Doves – Integrity and Good Practice in Pastoral Care	157
11 Messy Moments – Unsought, Untamed, Unimaginable Encounters	176

Epilogue

12 The Paradoxical Pastor	191
Sources and Acknowledgements	195
Index of Scriptural Passages	196
General Index	199

List of Figures

Table 3.1	Erikson's eight stages of development	36
Figure 3.2	The U curve of transition	39
Figure 5.1	The U curve of loss	75
Figure 6.1	Rites of passage	98
Figure 7.1	An ecology of Christian pastoral care	121
Figure 8.1	The shape of pastoral conversation	133
Figure 10.1	The effect of the role on the personal self	160
Figure 10.2	The effect of the personal self on the role	161
Figure 10.3	The supervision continuum	163
Figure 11.1	Embracing the pastoral moment	179
Figure 11.2	Pastoral care as narrative interpretation	184

1

The Humble Pastor
Imagining Pastoral Care

Pastoral theology is the study of how and why Christians care. In essence, we find that this caring impulse is devastatingly simple. We love because God in Christ has first loved us. But what that love will entail, in all the deep and demanding outworkings of pastoral practice, can bear a lifetime of critical exploration and prayerful discovery. This study guide aims to provide some helpful accompaniment along the way.

The first thing that we must acknowledge, before embarking on any serious study in this area, is that caring in itself need not be terribly complicated. It is in the nature of most pastoral activity, in fact, to proceed by quite modest pathways, often bumbling along through chance encounters and half-understood exchanges towards some first glimpses of human hope and healing. A stance of humility, therefore, both intellectually and spiritually, seems to be an essential prerequisite for authentic pastoral care; and some of its finest practitioners may appear, on the surface at least, to be surprisingly untutored.

What status should we assign, then, to a field of study which is designated 'pastoral theology'? Is it a specialized discipline which is the proper province of highly trained academics and professional theologians? Can we stake out a critical body of pastoral expertise and advanced proficiency which will elevate caring to a standard above the level of the 'ordinary' Christian? Or is there, possibly, something of immeasurable value in the care of the 'amateur' – a word which originally meant *lover* before it came to mean *unskilled* – whose unassuming compassion authentically reflects the humble generosity of a gracious God? We shall do well to stay grounded in humility as we take upon ourselves any formal study or ministry in the field of pastoral care.

This book is addressed to a readership that is both humble and also rather eclectic. Some readers may be approaching pastoral theology as part of their formal training for ordained ministry in the Church. For them, the expectations of an official and representative role will powerfully shape an emerging vision of pastoral integrity which they seek to embody in their vocation. Others, inhabiting a place amid the plethora of more or less formally recognized lay ministries in the churches, will be reading this book in the context of a role which is not so easy to define or delimit, but whose vocational expectations may be no less searching or profound. Still other readers, sensitive to the pastoral dimension of the whole of human life, may be drawn to explore an area of personal study which promises not only to enrich their stock of human wisdom, but also to enlarge their resources of compassion as members of a caring Christian community. In reading and discussing this book, it will be helpful to remember the distinctive contribution that each particular vocational perspective may bring to the overall scope of our pastoral vision.

This study guide will invite a stance of humble curiosity in relation to a wide canvas of human knowledge. To this end we shall explore, at least in an introductory way, some of the rich insights gathered from a thoughtful appropriation of research in many fascinating fields of enquiry relevant to pastoral care. Traditional theology, in the sense of a serious study of the nature of the good news that calls us into relationship with a loving God, will be indispensible to all our considerations. But so also will be our excursions into the behavioural sciences, whose sophisticated accounts of human well-being in all its biological and cultural, psychological and social dimensions will shed much light on the subtle depth and detail of how the good news of God's love might be shared and experienced. Within this multidisciplinary enterprise of pastoral theology, while garnering a rich harvest of knowledge about the human condition from many quarters, we may never pretend to be specialists in all areas. The pastor always remains in an important sense a non-expert, who holds her learning humbly, never forgetting the profound mysteries that will always lie beyond her grasp.

This introductory book will promote, therefore, an ongoing agenda of humble learning and reflective practice. However experienced we may be as pastors, and however much the quality of our care may be appreciated by others, we shall recognize that the more proficient we become as ministers, the more essential it will be for us to develop our understanding and to deepen our pastoral integrity. What makes our caring theologically authentic? Is our pastoral practice coherent in both social and spiritual terms? And how faithfully does it witness to life-giving compassion and grace? Without anxious navel-gazing or an obsessive preoccupation with the methodologies of reflection, this book will invite a continual questioning of our theological presuppositions and a humble evaluation of practice.

With such challenges in mind, this book will not be shy about discussing prayer. It is one of the tragedies of much modern reflection on the many-faceted tasks of ministry that the cultivation of pastoral skills has sometimes been examined in isolation from any attention to the spiritual heartbeat which sustains them. Such functionalism is misleading and damaging. To be a Christian pastor is to dwell deeply, day by day, in the love of God. Our pastoral care draws its whole life and integrity, its orientation and sustenance, from a deep well of divine grace that flows in and through a personal and corporate life of prayer and worship. Nothing less than a quiet prayerfulness beneath and beyond our outward caring will plumb the depths of incarnational ministry which we are called, in Christ, to share. We shall do well to pause often in our studies, as well as in our pastoral activities, to return humbly to the spiritual wellsprings of this ministry within the fathomless compassion of God.

These, then, are some initial pointers to the vision of pastoral theology which we hope to inspire through this study guide. Pastoral theology is a challenging and deeply illuminating field of study which will stretch and enlarge the humble student on many levels. At the heart of its agenda is an intuition about God's passionate care for his people and his call to men and women, individuals and communities to a fullness of human life far beyond our imagining. It is to this overwhelming promise of covenant love that we turn our attention as we now proceed.

A steadfast commitment to care

We love because he first loved us. (1 John 4.19)

Deeply inscribed within the collective imagination of the Christian Church is a vision of the steadfast love of God. Weaving through the stories of countless men and women in the scriptures, across the ages and down to the present day, we trace a perennial witness to God's faithful loving-kindness, which is called in Hebrew *hesed*, or covenant love (Ps. 136). It is this love, streaming forth from the heart of the Trinity, which calls human beings into responsive relationship with God and caring commitment to one another.

The unfolding drama of gracious love is fleshed out in narrative form, as story after story in the Bible attests to the abiding commitment of a divine carer who never abandons his own. From the dawn of creation, this covenantal pattern establishes God's care for the earth and the creatures he has made (Gen. 9.8–17). The covenant takes concrete form in God's call to a particular people, beginning with Abraham (Gen. 12—15) and through his descendants to the whole people of Israel (Ex. 19—24). Through oppression and liberation, through disobedience and bitter exile to healing and restoration, we see God sustaining and renewing his covenant relationship with those whom he had called. As a mother tenderly embraces her children, the divine carer gathers a great family of peoples to his heart of love (Isa. 66.10–11).

For their part, God's people are commissioned to work out their vocation as a covenant community, to choose life and to care faithfully for one another (Deut. 29—30). Despite failure and fecklessness, God's love for them remains unshaken; and it was from their own people that he raised up Jesus our Redeemer, in whom every hope of divine promise and human fulfilment is finally embodied (Heb. 8.6). Through the Spirit of the risen Christ his Church is now called to continue Jesus' ministry, living as his Body in the world and learning what it means to care in his name (Col. 3.12–17).

This covenantal character of caring which we learn from the ancient narratives of our faith is deeply embedded within a Christian pastoral imagination. The distinctive ways in which we envisage the practice of care are richly coloured by our sense of covenantal participation in the gracious *hesed* of the Holy Trinity, flowing out in unceasing compassion towards humankind. Some of these distinctives are of particular importance for our contemporary pastoral context and will be emphasized repeatedly in the course of this book, marking out the deepest framework of significance undergirding how and why Christians care.

First and foremost, the covenantal vision of pastoral care has a radically *theological agenda*, that will disrupt and challenge frames of reference which are purely humanistic. Anchored in the fathomless ocean of divine love, covenantal care is energized by the unbounded possibilities of new life that well up from a relationship with the living God, touching and transforming human lives at *kairos* moments of gracious opportunity for new freedom and forgiveness, healing and hope.

In the second place, a covenantal vision provides an emphatically *corporate outlook*, which subverts the narrowly individualistic perspective in which pastoral care is portrayed as a balm for primarily personal ills. The mutuality of love, so powerfully reflected in the grace of God in Trinity, summons Christian people not merely to individual fulfilment but to an outward-facing concern, one for another, which strains towards full maturity through relationships of openhearted communion and unstinting justice.

A third emphasis of the covenantal vision, which is in radical contrast to modern contractarian attitudes, is the wholeheartedly *personal investment* which underlies the costly enactment of Christian care. This self-involving commitment must critique any detached model of professionalism, which presents caring in terms of predominantly technical competence and skill. The gospel of Jesus, grounding our whole ministry within the sacrificial soil of self-giving love, commits his disciples to far-reaching participation in his humble compassion and suffering service.

These are the characteristics of God's steadfast covenantal commitment which shape and sustain a theological vision of pastoral care. Christian pastors are called to contemporary participation in an age-old passionate exchange of love between God and his people and to discover, through grace, their own particular contribution to the humble outworkings of love's day-by-day demands.

Thinking about care

How might this care begin to take shape? While a great deal of tender loving care is enacted at purely intuitive levels of human functioning, it is no disrespect to our basic capacity for compassion to try to examine more critically the fundamental components of caring attitudes and behaviours. To analyse care in a multidisciplinary way, we can start with the insights of philosophy and psychology.

Philosophers approach care by seeking to articulate the structures of meaning by which human beings understand the phenomenology of care. Psychologists probe more deeply the processes through which compassion might be enabled, or blocked, amid the complex interactions of day-to-day relationships. Using such tools of critical analysis can help us to engage in conscious reflection on practices which, while to some extent deeply innate, can be susceptible to more rigorous ongoing development.

One of the most influential modern philosophers of care was Milton Mayeroff, whose short monograph *On Caring* (1971) offers a beautiful survey of this sensitive area. Excavating the inherent rationality of human caring, Mayeroff drew out eight elemental aspects which resonate quite profoundly with the Christian narrative of covenantal love. On this account caring is rooted in *devotion*, demanding a *knowledge* of the other, which is integrated with further attributes of *humility*, *patience*, *honesty*, *trust*, *reflexivity*, *hope* and *courage*.

Mayeroff traces the solicitous character of care in delicate detail. *Knowledge*, for example, is envisaged not merely as an objective or 'clinical' appreciation of another person's situation, but as an ability to discern 'from inside' what the other person experiences or requires to grow. The *devotion* which undergirds the particularity of genuine care for another person involves 'being there' for them with trustworthiness and courage. But Mayeroff understands that this cannot be the same as 'being with' someone at every point along the road. There is a rhythm of caring which requires phases of closeness and of detachment, in order that genuine growth and freedom might be sustained without being smothered. It is for this reason, perhaps, that caring demands above all a humble trust that the other will grow to maturity in their own way and in their own time.

Pastoral Story

Kelly was experiencing a difficult adolescence. In the wake of her father's early death, Kelly's mother faced an immense struggle to cope with the burden of single parenting alongside her own overwhelming grief. The ensuing battle with chronic anxiety and the low level of family income made home life tense and uncertain. For young Kelly, her whole experience of childhood was scarred by profound insecurity and loss.

People in the local church knew of the family's situation. Following her husband's funeral, the vicar had invited Jan, Kelly's mother, to the Mother-and-Toddler group, where she made some good friends. Together, these young mums had been unobtrusive in keeping an eye

> out for Jan and trying to lend a hand whenever possible in caring for Kelly.
>
> Kelly herself thought that church people were rather 'sad'. At the age of 12, she was spurred by the incentive of extra pocket money to join the choir, but found all talk of God and Jesus painfully embarrassing. She came to like the friends she made at church, however, and tagged along with the close-knit group of teenagers in the youth fellowship. The youth pastors were patient with Kelly's outbursts of attention-seeking behaviour, making room for her to grow through warmth and encouragement, while praying that she might come to shed her awkward self-consciousness in a steadily supportive environment.
>
> She could not put it into words at the time, but Kelly began to feel respected and understood. When she was invited to be a bridesmaid for a cousin's wedding, it was her mother's friends from a Christian family who offered some help to pay for her outfit, and one of the youth pastors who accompanied a nervous 14-year-old to her first ever visit to a beauty salon. When Jan saw Kelly's beaming confidence as she walked through the church on the day of the wedding, it was the first time in years that she felt happy and proud to be her mother.

A psychological account of caring adds further insights into subtle interpersonal processes. We can examine the dynamics of compassion, for example, in terms of its emotional characteristics and the way these affective responses play out in cognitive ideas and interactional behaviour. A subjective experience of tender-hearted concern may be evoked by perceptions of the other as being in some way vulnerable, for example, or responsive to a personal identification with dependency and need. Such caring feelings and the physical stirrings which accompany them are inextricably bound up with an empathic imagination, which discerns the particular quality of suffering that calls out a caring response. The accuracy of these perceptions in turn, married to a motivation arising from felt concern, can shape an appropriate caring response which is directed towards the effective support and relief of the one who is having a difficult time.

This kind of psychological analysis is instructive in relation to the links between compassion and spirituality, suggesting how a prayerful capacity for attentiveness might encourage deeper and more sustainable resources of caring.

In a similar fashion, the links between compassion and cognition can help to inform the intellectual frameworks of effective counselling theory.

Further important insights about the processes of compassion emerge from recent studies by feminist scholars who give special emphasis to the corporate nature of caring and the intrinsic reciprocity in everyday enactments of pastoral care.[1] This kind of focus shifts beyond the one-to-one commitment of more or less skilful individual carers to encompass the more complex give-and-take of holistic caring communities. Rejecting any dangerous pretensions to being the powerful 'one-caring' in the face of a vulnerable 'cared-for' other, feminist scholars invite a richer practice of care which looks beyond individual professional expertise towards the inter-personal adventure of more messy human relationships.

Within this radically corporate vision of caring, the risks of mutuality and whole-souled involvement are embraced within a resilient web of care, the strength of which becomes far greater than the sum of its individual threads. Within church life, a story such as that of Kelly illustrates the combined power of shared lives and conversations, coffee clubs and choir practices. It is in these everyday exchanges of care that Christians learn what it means to bear one another's burdens (Gal. 6.2). As joys and sorrows are woven together through the organic attachments of interdependent relationships, each child of God can find a secure place to become more responsive, more human and more whole.

'The pastor in the mind'

We can begin to think more clearly about caring relationships using the precise tools of philosophical and psychological analysis. But for a deeper exploration of the sources of pastoral behaviour we also need to take into account those hidden and inchoate factors which work below the conscious level. There are many deeply primitive intuitions which strongly colour the ways in which human caring is experienced and practically understood. To unearth these deep-seated archetypal imaginations is a crucial additional task for pastoral theology.

---

1 See, for example, Carol Gilligan, 1982, *In a Different Voice: Psychological Theory and Women's Development*, Cambridge: Harvard University Press; Nel Noddings, 2003, *Caring: A Feminine Approach to Ethics and Moral Education*, Berkeley, CA: University of California Press, original edition, 1984; and Barbara McClure, 2010, *Moving beyond Individualism in Pastoral Care and Counselling: Reflections on Theory, Theology and Practice*, Eugene, OR: Cascade Books.

It is commonly recognized that people project certain ideals and expectations onto caring figures, especially those in public roles like members of the clergy. We may be less aware, however, of the ways in which those people in caring roles are themselves affected by the inner ideals and expectations which they carry around, like so many baggage labels, in their own minds. More or less consciously, some ideal image of 'the pastor in the mind' plays out in the archetypal imagination of individuals and churches, profoundly affecting the behaviour of Christians who give and receive pastoral care.

We need to consider that some of our treasured images of ministry might be dangerously misleading: sentimental idols of the mind which obstruct the authentic purposes of fully Christian care. One of the important tasks of pastoral theology, therefore, is to deconstruct some of these internal working models and subject them to careful critique.

The classic inherited image of the pastor as shepherd of the flock, in particular, has come in for some sharp iconoclastic criticism in recent years. Is our imagination of the caring shepherd anything more than a nostalgic vestige from a romanticized agrarian past which carries little resonance for a modern urbanized society? Worse than that, does the image of a strong and manly shepherd set up hierarchical expectations which are patronizing to those in his care, especially for significant numbers of women? Perhaps the aura of such a potent 'pastor in the mind' perpetuates an unhealthy clericalism in parts of the Church, setting up expectations of all-competent ministers who expect (and are xpected) to be 'in charge' of their lay, dependent and unintelligent 'sheep'. A critical examination of our guiding images might save us from ego-inflated idols, which are demeaning to those for whom we are called to care.

But it is important not to take our deconstructions too far. The same scriptures that carry stark warnings to those 'shepherds' whose high calling is vitiated by self-interest (Ezek. 34.7–16) also point us towards the supreme embodiment of good shepherding in the ministry of Jesus (John 10.1–16). Pastoral theology at its constructive best will enrich and inspire through a whole fund of images which both critique and expand a vividly Christian imagination of the possibilities of care. Robert Dykstra, for example, sets alongside the ideal of the solicitous or courageous shepherd the more paradoxical images of the 'circus clown', the 'wounded healer', the 'wise fool' or the patient 'midwife' (2005).

Reconstructing and refreshing 'the pastor in the mind', in a world of confusing and often conflicting expectations of Christian ministry, becomes an essential discipline for the nurturing of deep-rooted integrity and pastoral wisdom. If we can dare to be honest about the pious pretences that sometimes possess the imagination, then we might begin to develop not only a proper humility about our calling, but also a good-humoured sense of godly perspective.

> ### A Pastoral Prayer
>
> O Good Shepherd Jesus
> good, gentle, tender Shepherd,
> behold as a shepherd, poor and pitiful,
> a shepherd of your sheep indeed,
> but weak and clumsy and of little use,
> cries out to you.
> To you, I say, Good Shepherd,
> this shepherd, who is not good, makes his prayer.
> He cries out to you,
> troubled upon his own account, and troubled for your sheep...
>
> And you, sweet Lord,
> have set a person like this over your family,
> over the sheep of your pasture.
> Me, who take all too little trouble with myself,
> you bid to be concerned on their behalf;
> and me,
> who never pray enough about my own sins,
> you would have pray for them.
> I, who have taught myself so little too,
> have also to teach them.
> Wretch that I am.
> What have I done?
> What have I undertaken?
> What was I thinking of?
>
> Aelred of Rievaulx (1110–67)[2]

---

2 Aelred of Rievaulx, 1971, *Treatises and the Pastoral Prayer*, Kalamazoo, MI: Cistercian Publications, pp.105, 107.

A humble calling

How and why do Christians care? As we embark on our studies in pastoral theology, we shall expect to think more rigorously and more deeply about the links between theory and practice in ministry. We shall also be encouraged to attend to the inner dispositions of the heart which work to sustain and nourish our tentative adventures of covenantal love.

But throughout this chapter we have intimated that it is primarily a disposition of humility, both intellectual and spiritual, which is the fundamental prerequisite for pastoral care in the spirit of Christ. A few final comments will ground this central assertion and sketch the beginnings of a manifesto for the Christian vocation in terms of being human, being there and being good news.

Being human

Before anything else pastors are called to be human. This is because real human life, raw human compassion and a passionate commitment to human salvation – these things lie at the heart of the Christian doctrine of incarnation. Wherever pastoral care is practised in the pattern of Christ it will be earthed, therefore, in a full-bodied experience of human life, which begins with the lived humanity of those who are its practitioners.

This means that the education of pastors involves first and foremost an attention to their own humanness. Being utterly human and not shrinking from the depth and complexity of that humanity is a primary qualification for those who seek to walk with others on the road towards the full human dignity of children of God. We must expect that the study and practice of pastoral theology will raise core questions about that humanness, in all its mess and glory. The humble pastor must remain utterly grounded, embracing life's questions and working out a Christian maturity which stays faithful to her own rich and troubling humanity.

Being there

The crucial corollary of incarnation is presence. Simply being there, in all the fullness and fragility of shared human presence, contributes far more in terms of pastoral care than any number of skills and competencies and theoretical sophistications. Of course, this is not to suggest that a sensitive pastoral presence will not be enhanced by the development of academic insight and practical wisdom. But it would be seriously wrongheaded to imagine that pastoral effectiveness is ultimately commensurate with professional or intellectual cleverness.

Pastoral care requires availability. Being there, for and with the other, in the steadfast immanence of covenant love is itself a presencing of the gospel, a tangible expression of the immediacy of God's love and the nearness of his grace, through the extended ministry of incarnation which Christ has entrusted to his Church.

Needless to say, the extent and scope of that presence and availability must be governed by a wise humility. No individual and no church can offer total availability and unfailing attention. That would be a reckless misunderstanding of the call to Christlike compassion. We shall discuss in later chapters the importance of boundaries in pastoral practice; but we might notice at this point that a humble and deliberate limitation of presence and availability is not at all inconsistent with a deeply generous investment in those small everyday responses and relationships which, along with the part that others have to play, weave together in a faithful web of genuinely incarnational care.

Being good news

'See how these Christians love one another!' Tertullian, one of the earliest apologists for the faith, described how the quality of care within and beyond the Christian community was so exceptional that even scornful pagans were impressed at what they saw. Their humility and kindness towards one another, not to mention their generosity towards any who were in need, was the distinguishing badge of disciples whose manner of life gave such powerful testimony to the gospel.

It is a pity that subsequent generations of Christians have sometimes disregarded or downplayed the significance of pastoral care, as if this witness is somehow in competition with other vitally important missional priorities such as evangelism or church leadership or preaching and teaching the good news of God's love.

The integrity of pastoral theology is rooted in a thoroughly holistic understanding of the gospel, which is meaningless as a belief structure unless it is embraced as a transformative vision for everyday life. The good news of God's passionate love for every human being is something which pastors are invited to taste for themselves and to work out in openhearted commitment to those for whom they are called to care.

Towards that end, this book offers a humble overview of a rich and glorious field. The first part paints a picture of *Life in all its Fullness*, sketching out some key dimensions of the call to true humanity which is central to the gospel. We shall brood over the deep questions of being human, for ourselves and for one another, aware that for all our study we shall only begin to know in part something of the fullness of glory to which God's love eternally invites us (1 Cor. 13.12). Part 2 directs our gaze outwards in response to the practical call to care, *For Their Sakes* (John 17.19). We shall examine the understated genius of a classically British model of pastoral care, whose integrity lies in a modest refusal of false professionalism in favour of the simpler pastoral virtues of good listening, wise counsel and a respectful attention to balance and boundaries.

Humbly confident

It is not unusual in the classified sections of the church press to find smartly designed advertisements for ministers who are 'dynamic' or 'innovative' or 'visionary'. Very rarely does the vital pastoral quality of 'humility' top the list of desirable characteristics for someone offering service in the Church! This book puts the countercultural idea that we need to reclaim the wisdom of humility as a guiding virtue for the orientation of pastoral care in the spirit of Christ. This is in no way to commend timidity or lack of conviction. On the contrary, we shall see that it is precisely the humility of the pastor which fosters real confidence in her role. This is the paradox of a calling which seeks nothing less than a wholehearted embrace of the human condition, in all its brokenness as well as all its glory, and it is a vital charism for the recovery of good news in our times.

Questions

For private journaling or prayerful reflection

- What ideal images do you carry of 'the pastor in the mind'?
- To what extent do these images encourage or undermine an attitude of pastoral humility?

For group discussion

- What expectations of pastoral care have you encountered, both inside and outside the Church?
- How do these expectations and understandings compare with your own Christian vision of pastoral care?
- How might you apply these insights to the care of someone like Kelly?
- What are the tensions between a proper professionalism and a gracious humility in Christian pastoral practice?

Further Reading

Campbell, Alastair V., 1985, *Paid to Care? The Limits of Professionalism in Pastoral Care*, London: SPCK.

Countryman, L. William, 1999, *Living on the Border of the Holy: Renewing the Priesthood of All*, Harrisburg, PA: Morehouse Publishing.

Dykstra, Robert C., 2005, *Images of Pastoral Care: Classic Readings*, St Louis, MS: Chalice Press.

Hunsinger, Deborah van Deusen, 2006, *Pray Without Ceasing: Revitalizing Pastoral Care*, Grand Rapids: Eerdmans.

Mayeroff, Milton, 1990, *On Caring*, New York: HarperCollins, original edition, 1971.

Moody, Christopher, 1992, *Eccentric Ministry: Pastoral Care and Leadership in the Parish*, London: Darton, Longman and Todd.

Pattison, Stephen, 2000, *A Critique of Pastoral Care*, London: SCM.

Scott, David, 1997, *Moments of Prayer*, London: SPCK.

Tidball, Derek, 1997, *Skilful Shepherds: Explorations in Pastoral Theology*, Leicester: Apollos.

Wells, Samuel and Sarah Coakley (eds), 2008, *Praying for England: Priestly Presence in Contemporary Culture*, London: Continuum.

Part 1

Life in all its Fullness: The Call to be Human

2

Being Human

Life, Love and Longings

At the heart of the Church's pastoral ministry is a compelling theological vision of what it means to be human and what it takes to care. Unlike many shallow and unsatisfactory accounts of human existence, this Christian vision extends a deep and challenging invitation to respond to our calling as people created, loved and healed through the boundless grace of God. In this chapter, we shall outline the foundations for pastoral wisdom in a theological anthropology which offers a distinctive account of the human condition – in all its life, love and longings – measured by nothing less than the full stature of Jesus Christ.

Theology and pastoral care

What does it mean to be human? The question is not merely theoretical. All of us shape our own lives and relate to the lives of others on the basis of some deep, tacit understandings of human life and existence. Our sense of dignity, our sense of purpose, how we invest our time and our talents and the way we struggle with our fears and frustrations, all reflect core underlying assumptions about what it means to be truly human.

In the wisdom writings of the Bible, the question of human nature is always framed by a sense of the ultimate sovereignty of God: this is what we mean by theological anthropology. Psalm 8, for example, records a beautiful hymn which celebrates the profound dignity accorded to human beings by their Creator. The opening cry of praise, 'O Lord our Sovereign, how majestic is your name in all the earth', which also closes the psalm, sets a majestic framework of

> **Psalm 8**
>
> O Lord, our Sovereign, how majestic is your name in all the earth!
>   You have set your glory above the heavens.
> Out of the mouths of babes and infants you have founded a bulwark
>   because of your foes,
>   to silence the enemy and the avenger.
> When I look at your heavens, the work of your fingers,
>   the moon and the stars that you have established;
> what are human beings that you are mindful of them,
>   mortals that you care for them?
> Yet you have made them a little lower than God,
>   and crowned them with glory and honour.
> You have given them dominion over the works of your hands;
>   you have put all things under their feet,
> all sheep and oxen,
>   and also the beasts of the field,
> the birds of the air, and the fish of the sea,
>   whatever passes along the paths of the seas.
> O Lord, our Sovereign,
>   how majestic is your name in all the earth!

reverence and awe within which the psalmist can celebrate the remarkable God-given vocation of human beings.

In terms of biblical wisdom, it makes little sense to speculate about the essential nature of humanity without first establishing a vision of the ultimate context in which human beings live and grow. With this in view, the psalmist focuses first and last on the praise and glory of God, before turning his attention to the unique calling of human beings with their special authority to order and care for God's world. Who and what we are as human beings and how we are to thrive amid all that human life entails are questions of profound pastoral importance, which cannot be satisfactorily answered by non-theological accounts of human nature. As we explore the principles of a distinctively Christian pastoral care, we shall return throughout this book to an underlying theological vision of the goal of human nature which is supremely grounded in the gift and call of God in Jesus Christ.

Life in all its fullness

'The glory of God is the human person fully alive', wrote Irenaeus of Lyons in the second century. Christians rejoice in the knowledge that, whatever the derangements and difficulties of human experience, individually and collectively, the purpose of God will be fulfilled in and through human flourishing. Nothing less is promised by Jesus himself who, in the words of the gospel writer, 'came that they might have life, and have it abundantly' (John 10.10).

> ## Pastoral Story
>
> Susie grew up with cerebral palsy. Her parents never knew for certain whether some carelessness had contributed to the lack of oxygen at birth, which damaged her infant brain, but they struggled to accept the implications of an irreversible disability which limited her physical and mental capacities, sometimes in ways which were very hard to comprehend.
>
> Susie had a lovely smile. Somehow the slight tilt of her head and the barely perceptible asymmetry of her face seemed to add to her charm. As she grew through childhood, friends and neighbours often commented on her 'sweet personality' and 'tremendous progress'. Yet, for Susie's parents, the harsh realities of her perennial clumsiness and her significant learning difficulty made all the everyday tasks of parenting more than usually complicated and overwhelmingly more exhausting.
>
> Of course, they were glad to be assured of the love and support of church friends. Their vicar went to great lengths to ensure that Susie could be included in all the regular opportunities of church life: singing with the children's choir and preparing for confirmation. But deep undercurrents of frustration and fear for the future tore at the heart of their family life, erupting in occasional outbursts of marital anger and seething in quiet outrage towards anyone who dared to suggest that God must have some uniquely special purpose in Susie's disability.
>
> *What might 'life in all its fullness' mean for Susie and her family?*

At the most fundamental level, Christians believe that the story of human nature is a story of God's blessing. Starting with creation, we affirm that our value and identity as human creatures is unshakably grounded in the creative purpose and delight of a loving Creator. Along with all other creatures, human beings owe their very existence to the goodness and generosity of God. 'The Lord is good to all, and his compassion is over all that he has made' (Ps. 145.9). Yet, the unfolding of the scriptural narrative introduces far richer insights into the relationship between our creator God and his human creatures. The astonishing testimony of the New Testament is that God himself came to share the life of his own creation, taking up the very nature of a human being in the incarnation of his Son, Jesus Christ: the Word became flesh (John 1.14). What is more, this eternal Word who was born into a human family went on to suffer and die for sinful humanity and, through his death and resurrection, to raise up human beings to glorious new life in God through the grace and power of the Holy Spirit.

This is the story of human destiny which Christians love to rehearse in praise of God the Holy Trinity. We rejoice in a covenant of faithful love which was established by God the Father in creation, which was sealed in the redeeming blood of Jesus his Son and which is being drawn to full consummation through the mighty and mysterious animating power of the Holy Spirit. It is within the unfolding beauty of this wondrous story that Christians learn to appreciate the unique dignity of the human vocation and to address with humble faith and hopeful anticipation the question of what 'life in all its fullness' might mean.

The shape of living

The particular vocation of human creatures is to enter into free and conscious fellowship and communion with God. Something like this seems to be suggested by the tantalizing biblical description of human beings fashioned 'in the image of God'. Not that human nature, in and of itself, is endowed with some special virtue that sets it apart from the rest of creation. The unique dignity of human creatures cannot be located in any identifiable strength or faculty of our own possession. It is rather to be found in our reflecting, and responding to, the glory of God who calls us into being and invites us to share the blessings of his eternal generosity and inexhaustible love. It is this gracious calling, to being-in-encounter with God and with one another, which underpins an authentically

Christian account of human nature and which guides a theological understanding of the contours of human living in the world.

We shall consider how this vision shapes a pastoral understanding of human experience in relation to four key dimensions: life in all its times and seasons; life in all its frustration and fragility; life in all its mutuality and communion and life in all its hope and potential.

Life in all its times and seasons

Human life is part and parcel of the natural world, and human beings are creatures of time. Each life is finite: in the poetic imagery of the psalms, we flourish 'like a flower of the field' (Ps. 103.15). Against the eternity of God, the humble span of human life is brief and beset by turbulence and change; yet it is by no means inconsequential or uncared for in the face of God's everlasting compassion (Ps. 90).

The picture that emerges from the tradition of the scriptures is a subtle and complex vision of a human span of life which is uncompromisingly finite, mortal and rooted in time, yet, which is also being haunted by a sense of eternity through mysterious and intimate relationship with God. In a passage of aching tenderness, the poet of Ecclesiastes reflects that God 'has made everything beautiful in its time. He has also set eternity in the human heart.' (Eccles. 3.11, NIV)

Here lies the paradox of human temporality which weaves its way through any serious account of pastoral theology. Human beings come to birth, live and grow, flourish and struggle and finally face death as creatures of time. Our days and years are numbered, and we pass through earthly existence with an inexorable sense of past and present pressing towards the future. Yet, within and beyond this relentless forward movement of *chronos* (clock-like, created time), human beings also sense a deep calling to know and respond to the eternal love of God which both transcends and mysteriously intersects with mundane time. Shot through the daily quotidian experience of time-bound earthly existence are glimpses of a divine, eternal sphere of reality, revealed to human beings in *kairos* moments of singular grace and unique opportunity.

One of these special moments came along when 12-year-old Susie took her first Communion. After years of feeling on the edge of things, the day came when Susie took her place alongside other younger and older church members to receive for herself the sacrament of Christ's love. As she held out her hand for the bread and the wine, her smile was radiant. She knew she was included. She felt God's blessing deep in her heart. And despite all the difficulties and delays in her physical and mental progress to this point, Susie at last could taste and receive the assurance of divine kindness that would sustain her into adult life.

Through all the times and seasons of life, Christians believe that God's love beckons us towards life in all its fullness. This rich vision of God-shaped time has profound implications for a pastoral approach to human life.

- We affirm the sheer, inherent goodness of earthly life which is set within all the rhythms and relationships of the biological and cosmological created order (Gen. 1.31).
- We can know the faithfulness of God, through all the changing times and seasons of life (Ps. 34.1).
- With Christ, we are called to embrace every stage of human life as beloved children of God (Luke 2.52).
- In the ordinary course of life, for individuals as for peoples and nations, we are alert to those particular moments when the beckoning voice of God breaks through (Gen. 12.1; Mark 1.11; Ps. 95.7).
- The narrative shape of the Bible invites us, in all the twists and turns of life's pilgrimage, to recognize and respond to the love of God – for his steadfast love endures for ever (Ps. 136).
- In the midst of life, we are in death. As mortal creatures, all human life is lived on borrowed breath (Gen. 2.7).
- In Jesus Christ, God promises the gift of resurrection to a glorious new life in God's eternity (1 Cor. 15.22).
- The coming of Christ into the world, embracing our full humanity through his life and teaching, death and resurrection, signifies a crucial point in human history when the deepest purposes of God the Father begin to be disclosed (Gal. 4.4).

Ministers are privileged to care for people at key points in time, often coming alongside individuals and communities at moments of major transition. We shall explore further in Chapter 3 how a theological understanding of life in all its times and seasons provides a deep foundation of pastoral wisdom for supporting and guiding people at the crucial threshold points of human life.

Life in all its frustration and fragility

If there is wisdom in coming to terms pastorally with human finitude, then Christians also have profound insights to bring to the experience of human frailty.

One essential aspect of theological anthropology is its positive valuation of the whole created person and especially the human body. Unlike some classical views of human nature which are informed by Platonic rather than biblical understandings, Christians reject any dualistic separation between material and immaterial or between 'body' and 'soul'. Human beings relate holistically to God and to one another, and it is in the intimate unity of our embodied souls and our ensouled bodies that we come to know ourselves created, loved and healed by God.

It is important to affirm this essential unity of human nature, as we think about how to face up to the frustration and fragility of bodily life. Without a fundamentally positive appreciation of human embodiment, it would be tempting to locate all the sinfulness and struggle of human experience in a brutish 'lower' nature and to seek redemption through some spiritualized pursuit of a 'higher' form of life. This is a serious mistake which can lead to painful pastoral consequences.

In the unfolding narrative of Christian faith, we read of a good creation which is lovingly held in being despite its inevitable vulnerability to change and decay (Ps. 103.13–14). We encounter the astonishing story of a Saviour who entered the world in humble, human form, not evading the tragedies of human life, but giving himself to live and die as a man of sorrows, acquainted with grief (Isa. 51.3). And we hear the mysterious promise of human nature ultimately redeemed from the threat of destruction through the power of the Spirit, who raised Jesus Christ from the dead (Rom. 8.11).

These are the great truths of Christian theology which give strength and direction to pastoral care in the face of human suffering. Pastors recognize that it is often in the midst of fearful frailty and failure that human beings seek out their deepest spiritual resources. A child is born with a disability. A family faces the loss of a breadwinner. A community is devastated by sudden tragedy. It would be terribly easy to respond to such events with pious platitudes and well-meaning words. But rather than pontificating about affliction as an abstract challenge to human happiness, the power of Christian faith is tangibly revealed wherever communities learn to reach out in forgiveness and healing, hope and practical care.

For Susie and her family, the experience of bodily frustration and fragility was a daily reality throughout her growing years. It was pastorally immensely affirming, therefore, to find that fellow church members were willing to work around Susie's initial awkwardness with other children. They were determined not to exclude her from the group that was preparing for confirmation, even though some major adjustments in learning had to be made on Susie's account. By accepting and working with the inevitable frustrations and fragilities of Susie's disabled body and mind, these Christian friends and neighbours bore witness to the hospitality and healing power of the Body of Christ.

Life in all its mutuality and communion

In contrast to many contemporary secular accounts of human nature, Christians insist that human flourishing must never be conceived as an individualistic project – since human beings were made for relationship. Individual autonomy, individual progress, individual choice, individual achievement, individual wealth can never add up to a truly human dignity and maturity.

A theological anthropology takes its bearings from the inviting vision of being-in-encounter which we see in God the Holy Trinity of love. Human beings created in the image of this trinitarian God find their truest natural fulfilment in loving mutuality with each other and with other creatures, and their deepest spiritual identity in free and joyful communion with God. We are made, not for a life which is narrowly centred on our own sense of individual entitlement, but for an ex-centric existence which finds its richest significance and truest integrity through an open, loving exchange of grace with other persons in faithful community. Christians describe this as incorporation into the Body of Christ (1 Cor. 12.27).

One of the most exciting developments in recent theological study has been the wealth of fresh reflection on the doctrine of the Trinity. Far from portraying the inner life of God as some kind of complicated quasi-mathematical puzzle, contemporary theologians are rediscovering the outgoing movement of love which flows from the heart of the Trinity through the whole created realm. This gracious dynamic of love, which impels the Father to send the Son and to bequeath the Spirit, returns full circle to the bosom of God in a beckoning summons of invitation to human beings, who are called in God's image to intimate participation in the grace and power of divine life (John 17.22–23).

This reassertion of communion and mutuality at the heart of our understanding of God's nature has fascinating parallels with recent developments in academic research and reflection on human nature. From neuroscience to linguistic theory, from developmental psychology to systems theory, scientists and philosophers are re-emphasizing the communal dimensions of human experience. Politically and socially, sexually and emotionally, linguistically and culturally, we are learning that to become fully human is to grow in and through a web of rich and complex inter-relationships which mould and sustain our identity for an irreducibly corporate maturity. We shall explore these dynamics in more detail in Chapter 4 and Chapter 6.

Meanwhile, our reflection on Susie's human experience reminds us that relationality is a very practical key to pastoral understanding. Whatever joys and challenges Susie encounters in life will be faced within deep-felt bonds of personal and family ties of relationship. Her experience of faith will be nurtured within the potentially clumsy, yet caring initiatives of a local church congregation. The capacity of her family to cope and go on coping with the added demands of her disability will be held by an undergirding network of friends and teachers, babysitters and Sunday school teachers, with all the intricate relationships of extended family and everyday neighbourliness which, woven together, will assist in the bearing of a burden too heavy for individual parents to sustain.

If mutual relationships of love represent such a crucial dimension of human flourishing, then it is equally important to recognize the terrible impact of all that damages our openness to love – leading to frustration rather than fullness of life. From a pastoral perspective, arguably the most cogent insights into human sinfulness come from considering the multifarious distortions of human experience that arise where love, for whatever reason, is rejected.

Sometimes, as in Susie's story, the anxious shadows of lovelessness are discernible even from birth. In her case, it was the nagging suspicion of obstetric negligence which fuelled feelings of doubt and resentment in parents who needed, even more than most, to draw strength from relationships of faithfulness and trust. Like many similarly afflicted parents throughout history, instead of seeking a deeper reliance on the grace of God, they found themselves casting around for someone to blame (cf. John 9.2–3).

It is not the purpose of this book to develop a detailed doctrine of human sinfulness. What is vital pastorally is to be alert to ways in which human narratives of loving care and community are interwoven with cruel disappointments, distortions and doubts. At those points, a theological anthropology which grounds all human life, love and longing in the ultimate context of grace draws richly from the unfathomable depths of forgiving love.

> Lord, make me an instrument of your peace.
> Where there is hatred, let me sow love.
> Where there is injury, pardon.
> Where there is doubt, faith.
> Where there is despair, hope.
> Where there is darkness, light.
> Where there is sadness, joy.
>
> Prayer attributed to Saint Francis

Life in all its hope and potential

A note of irrepressible joy is the final most distinctive mark of a Christian account of human flourishing. In the light of God's goodness, the shape of living is emphatically hopeful. For Christians, the final realization of life in all its fullness is seen in the face of Jesus Christ. He embodies for us the ultimate fruition of human life in all its potential and holds out before us a glorious hope of what we may yet become.

But what can we make of such a hope for someone like Susie? Clearly our contemporary notions of bright human 'potential' and trouble-free 'progress', which are so widespread in an aspirational society, may raise expectations that are far beyond her reach. We cannot reduce Christian hope to simple optimism about human physical and intellectual development. Yet, neither should we console one another with a purely spiritualized hope of some future happy destiny which, like a fairy tale, will somehow overturn the miseries and misadventures besetting this mortal state.

What we glimpse in the story of Jesus is something much more astonishing. The hope that Jesus brings has all the character of a glorious surprise. It breaks into the world as amazingly good news, often unexpected, always undeserved. When Christ comes among human lives and communities, the blind receive their sight, the lame walk, the lepers are cleansed, the deaf hear, the dead are raised and the poor have good news brought to them (Matt. 11.4). It is a wonderful foretaste of the final Kingdom in which all the promises of God will reach their conclusive fulfilment.

Meanwhile Christian hope retains something of a hidden, humble, paradoxical character. Amid all the unpredictable contradictions of a broken world, the Spirit of Christ breathes fresh possibilities of grace which work to transform our everyday reality in deeply creative ways, while always leaning forwards to something still greater – yet to be revealed.

This is the irresolvable tension which calls our humanity ever more eagerly towards our true fulfilment in Christ. Between ashes and glory, a profound dissatisfaction and aching for transcendence nurture our longing for things that last. Energized by faith and inspired by unimaginable love, our restless human spirits press on till they find their ultimate rest in God.

It is this eschatological orientation, above all, that sustains the art of pastoral care as an authentically theological ministry. Neither relying on secular techniques for the alleviation of human unhappiness nor dependent on immediate results for the justification of its effectiveness, the humble practice of Christian pastoral care in a troubled world points to the audacious promises of God as the final source of human confidence and joy.

Learning wisdom

What does it mean to be human? We have reflected on some of the profound dimensions of life in all its fullness arising out of the Christian narrative: life in all its times and seasons; life in all its frustration and fragility; life in all its mutuality and communion and life in all its hope and potential. These richly theological themes can guide our thinking about the outworking of pastoral care, teaching us more about our human vocation in Christ and leading us into a more faithful understanding and humble practice of pastoral wisdom.

It is important, however, not to exclude other sources of wisdom beyond a purely theological frame of reference. Pastoral theologians down the ages, and particularly from the mid-twentieth century onwards, have been quick to engage with the best learning of their day to provide the fullest possible account of human flourishing. This kind of interdisciplinary learning has strong theological warrant, not least in the example of Jesus himself who grew and developed in wisdom from his youth onwards (Luke 2.52), demonstrating the keenest insight and integration of psychological, political and spiritual understandings of human life.

There are also compelling practical reasons for exploring the wealth of contemporary research into human nature, particularly from the human sciences such as psychology. Wesley Carr has summarized the unfortunate results which may ensue when ministers cut themselves off from the fruit of wider fields of study and research.

- Pastors may lose contact with people to whom they are trying to minister, lacking any proficiency in the matters with which they are concerned.
- Religion becomes separated from everyday life if it is uncritically detached from other fields of penetrating scientific enquiry and reflection.
- The people among whom the churches minister begin to think that Christians do not speak their language, especially in a culture where a great deal of self-understanding is expressed in terms of psychological language.
- Finally, and very seriously, pastors themselves may lose contact with their own humanity if they neglect to learn deeply about the springs and sources of human behaviour.[1]

In this book, we shall make frequent reference to the insights of the human sciences, drawing especially from understandings of psychology, sociology and anthropology to inform our interdisciplinary accounts of human behaviour. In all this, it will be important not to depend unduly on scientific learning for our perspectives on human nature, as if these studies in themselves could furnish a comprehensive account of the human vocation without reference to theological reflection and critique. We shall keep in mind the overarching perspectives of theological anthropology which keep us from any over- or under-valuation of human life, pursuing instead a humble and reverent respect for human dignity, which finds its truest identity in the face of Jesus Christ.

---

1 Wesley Carr, 1997, *Handbook of Pastoral Studies*, London: SPCK, pp. 37–8.

At this point, it will be sufficient simply to mention some of the major conceptual frameworks which have been embraced by pastoral theologians. In so doing, we emphasize again that Christian ministers should not attempt to present themselves as experts in fields of study which are beyond their competence, but may nonetheless orientate their approach to pastoral care through a critically informed appreciation of the wisdom to be gained and deepened from a range of current non-theological areas of relevant enquiry.

Chief among these conceptual frameworks from the human sciences will be the insights of psychology. From the late nineteenth century, a rich and sometimes bewildering proliferation of psychological schools has strongly influenced scientific and popular thinking about the human condition. At best, these studies have complemented pastoral and theological wisdom, bringing powerful and evidence-based analyses to bear on the inner world of the human soul or psyche. At times, however, an unfortunately competitive stance has set psychologists in opposition to theologians, devaluing or dismissing the transcendent dimensions of the human spirit in favour of a reductive insistence on solely humanistic frames of reference. It is important for pastoral theologians and carers to remain alert to the secularist presuppositions which may limit the value of scientific frameworks, while being humble enough to engage constructively with the many critical insights which these frameworks can provide.

In this book, we shall be considering the contributions of developmental psychology arising from a psychotherapeutic tradition (see Chapters 3 and 4) and finding broad application in the practice of counselling and spiritual direction (see Chapters 8 and 11). We shall also draw from the wealth of research into attachment and loss which has brought deep sensitivity and wisdom to the practice of bereavement care (see Chapter 5) and explore some of the insights of dynamic theory which have been so fruitful in relating to family systems, communities and group (see Chapter 6). Further reading on these areas of psychology will be given in the relevant chapters, and some general introductions are referenced at the end of this chapter.

From time to time, we shall also touch on frameworks drawn from the related fields of sociology and cultural anthropology. People practising pastoral care, and especially those entrusted with the particular responsibilities of ordained ministry, have a great deal to learn from role theory and from critical understandings of power and authority. These areas of social psychology are introduced in Chapters 9 and 10. Finally, the substantial contributions to ritual studies gained, the field of cultural anthropology will inform our thinking about the richly creative field of worship and pastoral care (see Chapter 6).

'Where is wisdom to be found?' asks the book of Job (28.12). For pastors, an open spirit of enquiry is an invaluable tool for perceptive guidance and transforming care. Our longing to grow more deeply human, for ourselves as much as for those among whom we will minister, will be enriched by a multidisciplinary awareness which holds together a profoundly reverent sensitivity to theological wisdom with a keenly intelligent engagement with the learning of the human sciences.

The human vocation

The fundamental orientation of all Christian ministry, and particularly of the ministry of pastoral care, is towards the building up of the Body of Christ, so that all people may come to human maturity – measured by nothing less than the full stature of Christ (Eph. 4.14).

An appreciation of theological anthropology, which we have begun to outline in this chapter, helps us to locate the ministry of pastoral care as part of the ongoing mission of God, who reaches out, in and through the Church, to the human beings whom he creates, loves and redeems. This chapter has shown how it is the whole of our human existence – in all its life, love and longings – which is addressed by the gospel call to fullness of life. In the next chapter, we shall go on to consider the processes of change and growth which mark the road towards maturity and through which God calls his children onward to newness of life.

Questions

'The thief comes only to steal and kill and destroy. I came that they might have life, and have it abundantly.' (John 10.10)

- In your own experience of the Church's teaching and ministry, which emphases do you find to be most life-affirming?
- Are there any aspects of the Church's witness you have experienced as life-denying?

- As you consider your own calling to pastoral ministry, what do you most wish to communicate about the value of human life in all its fullness?

Further Reading

Boa, Kenneth, 2004, *Augustine to Freud: What Theologians and Psychologists Tell Us about Human Nature (and why it matters)*, Nashville, TN: Broadman & Holman.

Carr, Wesley, 1997, *Handbook of Pastoral Studies*, London: SPCK.

Faith and Order Group, 2005, *Christian Perspectives on Theological Anthropology*, Geneva: World Council of Churches.

Fiddes, Paul, 2000, *Participating in God: A Pastoral Doctrine of the Trinity*, London: Darton, Longman and Todd.

Louw, Daniel, 1999, *A Mature Faith: Spiritual Direction and Anthropology in a Theology of Pastoral Care and Counselling*, Louvain: Peeters Press.

McFadyen, Alastair, 1990, *The Call to Personhood*, Cambridge: Cambridge University Press.

Savage, Sara, Fraser Watts and Ruth Layzell, 2004, *The Beta Course*. Available from the University of Cambridge Faculty of Theology.

Savage, Sara and E. Boyd-Macmillan, 2007, *The Human Face of the Church: A Social Psychology and Pastoral Theology Resource for Pioneer and Traditional Ministry*, Norwich: Canterbury Press.

Watts, Fraser, Rebecca Nye and Sara Savage, 2002, *Psychology for Christian Ministry*, London: Routledge.

3

Faithful Change

Growth, Transition and Maturity

Life in all its fullness involves ceaseless exploration and change. For faithful disciples, the transitions and turning points of life furnish vital challenges for maturation and growth. In this chapter, we shall reflect on how the unfolding journey of human life can be embraced as a pilgrimage of hope. Pastors and ministers, who are privileged to accompany others along this pilgrim way, will be more effective guides if they know something of the territory involved. We shall introduce, therefore, some outlines or maps of growth and transition drawn from scientific studies of human development, considering how they might help us in our care of people at different points in their life story and what they might suggest to us about some of the deeper goals of Christian pastoral care.

Through all the changing scenes of life

There are countless stories of change and growth in the scriptures. Some particularly adventurous stories, such as the extended Joseph saga in Genesis 37—50, have immense popular appeal; while many other shorter and less well-known stories reflect theologically on key points of decision and development in the lives of individuals and nations.

Human beings throughout the ages have relished the power of storytelling as a way of weaving together a coherent sense of meaning, purpose and identity. The biblical writers often use narrative in this way to affirm their confidence in God's loving purposes through all the changing scenes of life. There is a poignant example in the reflective prayer of Psalm 71, where the psalmist looks back over a long life to recall the ways in which God's faithful love has shone through.

> Upon you have I leaned from my birth;
> it was you who took me from my mother's womb. (v. 6)
> Do not cast me off in the time of old age;
> do not forsake me when my strength is spent. (v. 9)
> O God, from my youth you have taught me,
> and I still proclaim your wondrous deeds. (v. 17)
> So even to my old age and grey hairs,
> O God, do not forsake me,
> until I proclaim your might to all the generations to come. (v. 18)

The idea of mapping the spiritual journey through life has a long pedigree in the Christian tradition. One of the most ancient examples is *The Ladder of Divine Ascent*, written by John Climacus in the seventh century, which draws on the classic image of Jacob's ladder to suggest that growth in Christian maturity must progress through steps or stages. Like the scriptural writers, Climacus teaches that spiritual development is not a passive process, but one in which Christians respond to the grace and help of the Holy Spirit in an ongoing movement from glory to glory (see also 2 Cor. 3.18; Eph. 4.15 and 2 Peter 1.5–8).

A similar concept of progression and hope is deeply embedded in modern psychological theories of human development. If we remember that the word 'psychology' derives from the Greek root, *psyche*, which is generally translated as 'soul' or 'inner life', then we shall appreciate that contemporary psychological accounts of human development share many concerns with those of the ancient spiritual masters, albeit without their explicitly theological perspective. It is not unreasonable, therefore, for Christians to pick up some of the best insights of secular learning for our own theological and pastoral purposes – in the manner which Augustine of Hippo rather cheekily described as 'plundering the Egyptians'. As we saw in the last chapter, though, it will be important to bring a critical theological understanding to bear on some of the presuppositions of non-theological models if we are to integrate their best insights within a faithfully Christian approach to pastoral care.

The essential insight which all pastors must address is that faith cannot be regarded as a static quality which will sustain human beings, without alteration or change, through all the shifting demands and experiences of life. On the contrary, it is precisely in the defining moments of challenge and change that faith most often needs to be rediscovered and often reworked, if it is to foster authentic human maturity. With this goal in mind, pastors seeking to understand the complex transitions which are common to human life have a great deal to learn from developmental psychology.

Learning from life maps

A marked rise in life expectancy in modern Western societies – averaging half a century more than in biblical times – surely contributes to our contemporary curiosity about the way personal development continues throughout the whole span of human life. But the idea of recognizable life 'stages' goes back much further in popular imagination, as we see for instance in Shakespeare's portrayal of the 'seven ages of man'.[1]

In the twentieth century, psychologists began to map out in great detail the characteristics of the different stages of life, focusing on the intense dynamics playing out within key relationships. Sigmund Freud, for example, speculated on the ways in which an infant's negotiation of the relationship with his mother generated certain patterns of fulfilment and satisfaction, which echoed down the years in all manner of subsequent relational behaviours. Freud's famous studies have been fiercely debated and criticized, not least for their provocative representations of the pervasive role of unconscious sexual impulses, but they remain deeply influential for their insights into the challenges of particular stages of life and for their emphasis on the way in which deep-seated patterns of relational struggle may have repercussions throughout life.

Building on Freud's approach, psychodynamic theorists have developed a number of frameworks of particular interest to pastoral theologians. One of these, attachment theory, has borne tremendous fruit in the understanding of

---

1 The famous speech by Jacques in *As You Like It*, Act 2, scene 7.

the bonding and breaking of intimate relationships; we shall consider this theory in relation to bereavement in Chapter 5. In the current chapter, we shall summarize the 'life cycle' theory of Erik Erikson, which maps out the development of human identity over eight psychosocial stages from infancy to adulthood.

Central to Erikson's map of the stages of development is the idea of a psychosocial 'crisis', or turning point, which can lead to enhanced or impaired development in the stages to come. It is important to remember that Erikson uses the term 'crisis' in a technically specific sense, rather than in the looser sense in which the word has been adopted in popular literature to describe, sometimes in overly dramatic ways, the well-known adolescent 'identity crisis' or the frequently misunderstood 'crisis' of midlife.

> **Pastoral Story**
>
> Jilly is a 20-year-old student, who comes along to events run by the university chaplaincy team. She is pretty and outgoing and enjoys the company of other Christian students. Jilly talks enthusiastically about her intense involvement in a large charismatic church, where she is currently training as a student leader. Although she has many church contacts and Facebook friends, it seems as if close friendships are an issue for her; and most of the other students she befriends have emotional problems such as anorexia and self-harm. As a student, Jilly is diligent and hard-working, often bringing her impeccably presented project work to show to interested adults. Jilly goes home at least once a week to see her parents. She texts her mother frequently during the day to reassure her that she is having a happy time.
>
> *What are the pastoral issues around Jilly's transition from adolescence to full adulthood?*

Erikson's intricate schedule for human development analyses the eight stages of infancy, early childhood, play age, school age, adolescence, young adulthood, mature adulthood and old age, within a grid or 'epigenetic ground plan', which suggests how the resolution of each stage's crisis is a necessary precursor to the challenges that follow. Foundational to his whole scheme, and of particular significance for spiritual development, is the crisis of infancy, which establishes a character of fundamental trust over mistrust. It can be salutary to realize, in the course of everyday pastoral care, the extent to which any individual's capacity for faith is inevitably coloured by their experience of close relationships, possibly from the very earliest stages of life. This core insight is further elaborated in the theories of attachment and security developed by John Bowlby and Donald Winnicott (see Chapters 4 and 5).

Table 3.1

Erikson's eight stages of development		
Stage of life cycle	*Psychosocial conflict*	*Emerging virtue*
Infancy	Basic trust versus mistrust: Being profoundly dependent on others, can I trust the world?	Hope
Toddler	Autonomy versus shame and doubt: As I begin to seize control in basic areas, is it OK to be me?	Will
Pre-school	Initiative versus guilt: Now that I can more freely exercise my will, both physically and emotionally, is it OK for me to take initiatives?	Purpose
School age	Industry versus inferiority: I am becoming aware of my peer group. Can I make it in the world of people and things?	Competence
Adolescence	Identity versus role confusion: I am self-conscious, wondering about myself and who and what I can identify with. Who am I? What can I be?	Fidelity
Early adulthood	Intimacy versus isolation: I am ready to share myself with others. Can I love? How much can I give myself, and is it worth the risk?	Love

Middle adulthood	Generativity versus stagnation: I have distinctive gifts and energies to pass on. Can I make my life count?	Care
Old age	Integrity versus despair: I try to take stock at the end of a long life, seeking overall meaning and evaluation. Is it OK to have been me?	Wisdom

As the life cycle proceeds, Erikson's life map helps us to appreciate how an ever-widening circle of relationships and responsibilities brings opportunities and challenges for a deeper maturity. In the case of a young student like Jilly, the typical struggles of adolescence to develop a clear personal identity through which to relate to the wider world may be undermined by an ingrained legacy of mistrust or inferiority from earlier developmental stages. One of the practical implications of understanding development from a life cycle perspective is the need to take a whole life perspective on pastoral episodes. In this light, we may appreciate how someone with an insecure sense of identity, like Jilly, could be especially helped by the collective reassurance of a Christian community as she gathers her personal and spiritual resources towards facing the challenges of entering upon adult life.

Models like those of Erikson help to inform more critically the gospel call to fullness of life in all its times and seasons. By filling out our understanding of the subtle dynamics of psychosocial development, we can learn to be more attentive to those *kairos* opportunities for transformation, which all human beings face as they make their way through shifting developmental challenges and life stages. For Christians, these defining *kairos* moments can be times of particular openness to the healing and forgiving grace of God, which reaches back into our legacy of accumulated sorrows and struggles, at the same time calling us onward to a deeper and fuller maturity in Christ. This complex interaction between human repentance, divine assistance and spiritual growth is one of the critical insights of the gospel, which can sometimes be overlooked in shallowly progressivist and non-theological accounts of human development.

While there are significant limitations in Erikson's stage theory of the life cycle, with its somewhat mechanistic presentation of human development and its rather attenuated conceptualization of redeeming grace there is, nevertheless, great wisdom in his emphasis on human maturation as a more than individual matter. Erikson's cyclic descriptions of human psychosocial networks extend far beyond the individual, or even the nuclear family, to encompass a holistic vision of intergenerational and intercultural relationships. In a particularly powerful image, he describes the 'cogwheeling' interactions playing out between old and young, young and old, as each generation helps to bring forward the maturation of the other. Such insights lend psychodynamic weight to the communal and intergenerational context of pastoral care in faith communities (cf. Ps. 145.4).

Beyond the interplay of psychological forces, however, there is still rather more to be said about the theological foundations of maturation and growth within the Body of Christ.

Maturity and meltdown

One of the searching questions for pastoral care relates to the personal cost of change and growth. Christians know that lasting spiritual maturity is not attained without struggle – a struggle that can be intense and painful and bewildering. For this reason, the cool scientific language of psychosocial development may be insufficient to describe a thoroughgoing work of penitential transformation which can feel like going through the refiner's fire (Ps. 66.10; Prov. 17.3). More importantly, any model which envisages change and growth as a purely existential phenomenon on the human plane might overlook the richly significant theological dimensions of the work of God's Spirit in human crisis and renewal.

Christians use vivid language to describe the depth of the paschal mystery which forms our faith. It is Jesus Christ himself, who calls us through baptism to share in his death and new life (Rom. 6.3–4). The road to spiritual maturity will not be an easy walk in the park: disciples must expect a kind of dying with Christ which entails pruning (John 15.2), refining (1 Peter 1.7) and radical conversion (John 3.6–7). Life in Christ is definitively shaped by his cross and resurrection; and it is within the redemptive force field of this profound mystery that Christians face the major crises of life with an attitude of ultimate hope and expectancy. This has enormous implications for pastoral care and for the rich resources of word and sacrament that may be offered, with appropriate sensitivity, to nourish and sustain Christian pilgrims along the way of transformation.

In the midst of human life, it helps to recognize that each spiritual turning point necessarily entails a kind of dying – to old securities, old ways of knowing and being. It is a common feature of many conceptual models to describe significant transitions in terms of a threefold movement. William Bridges, for example, in a widely adaptable model of situational change, describes how the dynamics of transition progress from an initial disorienting *ending* of an old reality, through a strange and formless *neutral zone* where the new reality has not yet taken shape, towards the birth of a *new beginning*. This threefold dynamic structure can be simply presented in the shape of a U curve.

Figure 3.2 The U curve of transition

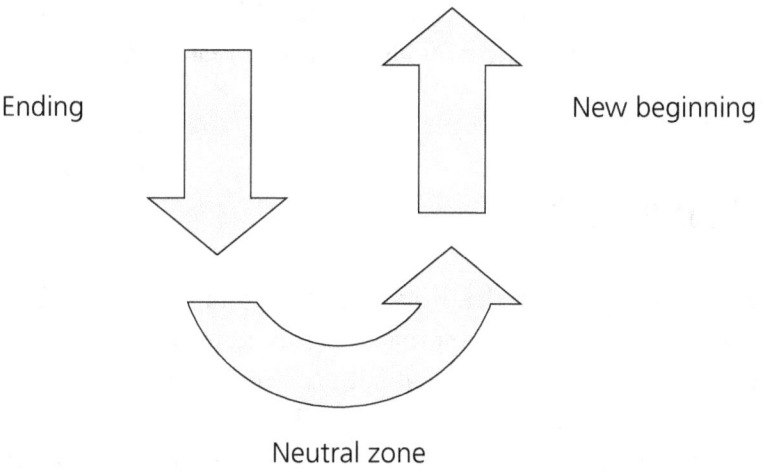

Organizational psychologists like Bridges[2] and Senge[3] emphasize the painful letting go, which must accompany the initial ending phase inaugurating any worthwhile transformation. With images redolent of religious meaning, the deeper individual and corporate work of transformation is often described in terms of meltdown or as an experience of death and rebirth or using the metaphor of traversing a barren wilderness.

For Christian pastors, this kind of imagery helps to connect the experience of transformation – whether situational or developmental – to the deeper goal of ministry which calls people into maturity in Christ. This is acted out week by

---

2 William Bridges, 1996, *Transitions: Making Sense of Life's Changes*, London: Nicholas Brealey.

3 Peter Senge, Joseph Jaworski, C. Otto Scharmer and Betty Sue Flowers, 2005, *Presence: Exploring Profound Change in People, Organizations and Society*, London: Nicholas Brealey.

week in the sacrament of the Eucharist, as God's people are schooled together in the dynamics of death and resurrection, which mould and sustain an ever deeper conversion to the way of Christ.

Whether the work of transformation relates to the predictable crises of human development, such as the end of childhood or the approach of old age, or to those unimagined interruptions of either trauma or joy, which disrupt individual and corporate life, the wisdom of faith invites us to discover in each recurring experience of transition a richer fellowship and deeper participation in the hidden mystery of Jesus' death and resurrection. Seen through the eyes of faith, our small crises are called into communion with the transforming paschal mystery of Christ's passion and glory. Pointing to this ineffable hope, the apostle Paul writes, 'You have died, and your life is hidden with Christ in God. When Christ who is your life is revealed, then you also will be revealed with him in glory' (Col. 3.3–4).

Faith development

Nowhere is this passionate mystery of death and glorification more telling than in the processes of faith development. In approaching this issue, we must appreciate that for some Christians the very idea that faith is something that develops over the course of life can be a little disconcerting. They have been taught to regard their faith as an unshakable rock – something which, once embraced, will hold them firm through the changes and chances of mortal life. Experienced ministers, however, recognize that some of the most demanding pastoral challenges arise from the seismic shifts that disrupt and destabilize the inherited faith of people in their care.

While it is true that the foundation for Christian discipleship is securely grounded on the rock of Christ (see Matt. 7.24–27), it is the universal experience of saints down the ages that our relationship with Christ calls us into a lifelong pilgrimage of growth which is initiated and sustained by the Holy Spirit (Heb. 12.1–2). Along this pilgrim way, we should expect to grow deeper in faith (2 Thess. 1.3; 2 Cor. 10.15), in love (1 Thess. 3.12), in the knowledge of God (Col. 1.10), in Christlikeness (Eph. 4.15; Gal. 4.19), in spiritual understanding and discernment (Rom. 12.2; Phil. 1.9), in obedience (1 Thess. 4.1), in grace (2 Peter 3.18) and salvation (1 Peter 2.2; Phil. 2.12–13). What we cannot expect is that this pilgrim's progress will be necessarily smooth or straightforward at every step along the way!

One of the most influential contemporary accounts of how faith develops through the course of life comes from the American pastoral theologian, James Fowler.[4] Fowler's research in this area began in 1972 and was much influenced by the work of earlier developmental stage theories including those of Erikson.

Fowler was curious to map the development of faith through the life course, and used empirical research to identify some of the universally recognizable stages which people of faith undergo. Before considering his findings in detail, it is important to note that his concept of this universal faculty of 'faith' has a particular construction. In his research context, 'faith' is regarded as the fundamental human capacity to make meaning out of life, which progresses emotionally and cognitively as people engage with changing personal and social contexts.

In practice, Fowler's model is judged by most pastoral theologians to be heavily weighted towards the cognitive dimension of how 'faith' comes to be understood. More nuanced understandings of faith as a story of a whole life pilgrimage may be less easy to break down into a simple stage model; yet despite some limitations it is clear that Fowler's tightly defined model has yielded some remarkably perceptive insights into faith development which have been very widely adopted in the Church. For this reason, it will be helpful to give an overview of his classic stage model.

Primal faith (Fowler's stage 0) describes how the capacity for trust and loyalty first takes shape in the pre-linguistic experience of the infant, who is nurtured within the matrix of primary caring relationships. We might even speculate that this stage of faith begins prior to birth as the child *in utero* gathers some sense of a welcoming and anticipatory cherishing or its opposite. This primitive form of faith, characteristic of infants but persisting as a foundation for all later faith, nourishes our first pre-images of God through the recognizing eyes and affirming smiles of parental figures. Fowler drew heavily from Erikson's analysis of the infantile crisis of trust versus mistrust to describe this most rudimentary layer of faith in which, at best, the seeds of a rich future spiritual life are first nursed into being.

Intuitive-projective faith (stage 1) typifies the awakening imagination of children who are beginning to use language. Sometimes called 'impressionistic

---

[4] James W. Fowler, 1981, *Stages of Faith: The Psychology of Human Development and the Quest for Meaning*, New York: HarperCollins.

faith', this stage is characterized by a profusion of images and symbols which evoke deep emotions, but with little sense of order. Consoling symbols, such as the image of Jesus the Good Shepherd, figure side by side with much darker images of cruelty and evil as the child encounters the contrasting emotions of ecstasy and terror, but without the conceptual or critical skills to evaluate them. For good and for ill, the vivid impressions gained at this early childhood stage will strongly colour the development of subsequent religious imagination. Even at much later adult stages of faith, the deeply evocative symbols of ritual and sacrament continue to speak to this immensely significant dimension of faith.

Mythic-literal faith (stage 2) describes the experience of children from around seven to twelve years of age, when the orientation to narrative and story becomes the dominant means of shaping and sharing meaning. Bible stories are very popular at this stage, though they will typically be interpreted in literal and one-dimensional ways. A sense of order is very important, even if this means that stories have to be forced into a neat shape, or rehearsed in a predictable fashion. While this approach may undergird a keen sense of moral coherence and a strong vision of narrative identity in school-age children, it is easy to see that the persistence of this style of faith in older people can be unhelpfully brittle and formulaic. In fact, from this point onward in his scheme, Fowler observes that not all young people and adults go on to embrace the later stages of faith development.

Synthetic-conventional faith (stage 3) is the style of faith commonly seen in adolescents, who are wrestling with the interpersonal dimensions of knowing and valuing. There is an acutely social perspective to the work of identity formation taking place at this stage, as the young person typically establishes a cluster of values and beliefs which are consistent with the norms of her supporting community. The young person's relationship to authority is, therefore, highly ambivalent. On the one hand, she has taken her first steps towards shaping a fully personalized faith and may be eager to express this sense of conviction through a public commitment of baptism or confirmation. Yet, on the other hand, what holds together her fragile faith-construction is an unrecognized dependence on other people and external sources of validating authority. The crisis marking the end of Fowler's stage 3 may occur when those supportive relationships and sustaining authorities begin to crumble.

> **Pastoral Story**
>
> Steve is a 30-year-old school teacher, who has been married to Rebecca for four years. Becca grew up in a Roman Catholic family supported by a network of close relationships centred on the church school, of which her father was the headmaster. Through the welcoming encouragement of his in-law family, Steve also came to embrace the Catholic faith, joining a catechetical class in preparation for his reception into the Church the week before their marriage. In the intervening years, a series of bitter events has buffeted his new-found faith. Becca's father, who had been such a strong role model for both of them, was diagnosed with terminal cancer. Three months after his death, Becca suffered the first of two miscarriages. And, just when the young couple most needed to lean on the support of a trustworthy church community, they were devastated to hear that their parish priest was being suspended for clerical misconduct. Steve has no words to describe the depth of his disillusionment with the Church and all that it stands for.
>
> *What are the challenges for pastoral care when someone's faith suffers meltdown?*

Individuative-reflective faith (stage 4) is adopted in and through critical self-awareness. This process may be far from comfortable as the maturing person faces some kind of emotional or spiritual 'leaving home'. In some instances, as Alan Jamieson has detailed, individuals find themselves leaving church for good.

What happens at this stage is that two important dynamic shifts occur. First, the individual becomes disembedded from the tacitly held beliefs, values and commitments of the earlier stage. With a critical distance from previous perspectives, there is space for questioning, critique and a deep grappling with issues of authority. Second, and more personally, the individual begins to embrace a new kind of personal authority and responsibility for the faith by which they live. They are no longer content to define themselves in terms of the family in which they grew up or the church community which shaped their faith. And, although continuing roles and relationships do not have to be broken at this point, it is not uncommon for more or less painful disruptions to mark the coming of age to a new kind of spiritual autonomy.

Fowler's depiction of this troubling stage of maturation casts a very helpful light on the tasks of pastoral care for growing Christians. A questioning faith can be tiresome and unsettling for those who feel more secure within the norms of belief and behaviour adopted by the church community. And church leaders can feel disappointed or undermined when individuals strike out in new and more autonomous directions. Perhaps Jesus' own example of patient support and appropriate challenge provides some clues as to how best to accompany disciples who are on their way to becoming strong leaders in their own right (cf. John 6.67–68).

Conjunctive faith (stage 5) describes a move to deeper complexity where the sharp-edged criticism of stage 4 is abandoned in favour of a more paradoxical understanding of faith in which seeming opposites are held together in loving tension and patient humility. The individual who worked so hard to achieve clarity and autonomy now faces up to his limitations, personally and intellectually. Sometimes through bitter experience, the individual must embrace the sacrament of defeat, learning a new receptivity to the goodness and truth of others and a deeper reliance on the mysterious grace of God. In this post-critical phase of integration, the believer may return with what Paul Ricoeur calls a 'second naivety' to the symbolic concepts and practices of an earlier faith: happy to acknowledge their partiality and provisionality, while being grateful to draw on their depth of healing power.

Fowler's snapshots of the later stages may be less well-defined than some of his earlier developmental vignettes because the empirical data from many of his subjects showed that adults often demonstrate a mixture of attributes from the different faith stages. It is uncommon to encounter a 'pure' stage 4 or stage 5 individual, and it may be unhelpful pastorally to expect to categorize people in this way. This is clearly the case in Fowler's final stage, which envisages an ideal point of maturity attained by very few individuals. It is said that Fowler drew from an interview with Mother Teresa and from his reading of other rare and saintly characters to sketch out a final point of symmetry in his overall scheme.

Universalizing faith (stage 6) describes the ultimate decentring of the self attained when the individual's circle of loving concern becomes so extensive that she finally empties herself out in a kenotic love, which is grounded in the universalizing goodness of God. In graphic terms, the figure of the individual is finally erased from the picture. Perhaps this saintly potential is foreshadowed in the most generative and profoundly simple aspects of each prior stage as the individual slowly learns to transcend self-preoccupation in complete, ex-centric abandonment to the surpassing mercy and wisdom of her Creator.

Fellow travellers on the road

The call to be human entails a faithful engagement with the whole pilgrimage of life – for individual Christians as well as for the mixed community of disciples, who travel together within and around the borders of church life. Pastors who seek to care for their fellow pilgrims must themselves walk as human beings and fellow believers along a challenging path of growth, transition and maturity, in which they are called not only to attend to their own development, but also to accompany their brothers and sisters along the way.

We need to be aware of the limitation of stage theories; but there is much that pastors can usefully take from their insights into human psychosocial and spiritual development to inform and encourage our Christian care for one another.

Problems with stage theories of change

In the first instance, we should be honest about the limitations. It is worth remembering, for example, that the very idea of identifiable 'stages' of faith is irritating to some believers. They sense, perhaps not unreasonably, that academics like Fowler are promoting certain ideal versions of 'faith' (possibly their own?), as if they were superior to other versions. This elitism is clearly at odds with Jesus' emphasis on the humility of faith and the necessity of childlike simplicity (Matt. 18.1–3).

There is also an inherent problem with stage theories which try to portray the complex vagaries of human experience through a structure which, on Fowler's own description, is 'invariant, hierarchical and progressive'. This is not to say that he regards the earlier stages of development as inferior versions of the real thing which will only be attained by the enlightened few, but rather that his structural theory aims to show how a certain faith stance, which may be no better or worse in terms of Christian faithfulness, is only possible after one has traversed and incorporated the perspectives of earlier stages. Despite this essential caveat, however, a lingering difficulty remains in the prescriptive tone of the model and the seemingly high valuations which Fowler places on the rationalist and individual dimensions of faith development, which may reflect a corresponding undervaluation of the development of more intuitive, or practical, or collaborative aspects of mature 'faith'.

In relation to pastoral care, we should be alert to the most serious problem of stage theories in their tendency to categorize and overdetermine immensely subtle and complex dimensions of human experience. A little knowledge of these categories can be a dangerous thing, as stage enthusiasts try to pigeonhole individuals or churches in ways which are far from pastorally sensitive or helpful. 'Of course St Peter's is such a typical stage 3 church. I don't expect they'll have much truck with your questioning there!'

Such broad generalizations about the growth of Christian maturity in individuals and churches are not only uncharitable, but they also conflict with a fully nuanced evaluation of their underlying research and, more seriously, with a theological conviction that all God's people are being called to a deeper conversion.

Pilgrims on a journey

The enormous strength of portrayals of faith development[5] is the seriousness with which they seek to understand and facilitate the challenges of deepening discipleship over the course of a whole lifetime.

For pastors, one of the sharpest insights of stage theories is that the points of transition, or stage changes, can be experienced as deeply disorientating, traumatic and troubling. We cannot envisage the development of faith as a gentle and undemanding stroll through life on the road towards a gradual and imperceptible maturation. On the contrary, along with many classic writers like John Bunyan, we recognize that the pilgrim path can be marked by alarming trials and radical upheavals.

There is a crucial role for pastoral care and leadership in this difficult terrain, calling for particular skills of discernment and sustaining wisdom. The guide

---

5 In addition to Fowler's scheme, other serious descriptions of faith development have been propounded by Robert Kegan and James Loder.

who accompanies pilgrims along the way needs clear maps and models, together with a commitment to walk alongside, to encourage and to help pace the onward journey.

This is never more important than at times of transition. The stage models which describe the structural elements of life and faith experience in almost architectural terms can help us to understand the enormity of the challenge undergone whenever that familiar structure is disrupted. A bereavement, a new job, a disillusionment with the Church, a new relationship: any inner or outer change can become the trigger for a major dismantling of those mysterious social and spiritual structures which hold people together. It is at these points that the sensitivity of individual and pastoral support is crucial.

The deep part of the U curve of transition can be a painful place of darkness and dislocation where the soul is lost in what T. S. Eliot described as 'the vacant interstellar spaces'.[6] When the whole architecture of a person's social, occupational, spiritual or emotional life is brought crashing down, then the sense of abandonment and grief can be utterly overwhelming. In some transitions, this is sudden and traumatic; other transitions may be slow and protracted, but no less bewildering for the person who has lost their bearings. The exquisite challenge of these periods of life, for any individual or community, is to face up to a deeper call to conversion.

In my end is my beginning

By the grace of God, within every crisis in the life of faith lies a promise of deeper maturity and integration. James Fowler indicates something of this conviction in his guiding image of the spiral staircase. Instead of portraying faith development as a series of discrete steps on a straight ladder, he takes a spiral staircase to reflect the familiar sense of returning to the same point time and again; yet, with each twist along the way finding that faith can be enriched by bringing more understanding and experience to incorporate.

Pastors with a good understanding of developmental dynamics need not be fazed by the spiritual disillusionments or the dramatic renewals, which often accompany traumatic transitions in the life of faith. God's covenantal mercy,

---

6 T. S. Eliot, 1969, 'East Coker', in *The Complete Poems and Plays*, London: Faber & Faber, p. 180.

which is the enduring theological foundation for all shifting human experiences in the life of discipleship, promises an ultimately faithful fulfilment in which many hidden seeds of faith will bear fruit for eternal life.

We have explored in this chapter some of the profound implications of developmental theory for a pastoral understanding of changing, growing and maturing human beings. While the detailed skills and knowledge needed for specialist work at particular periods of the life cycle lie beyond the scope of this book,[7] the key principles of faithful, expectant accompanying provide rich resources for pastoral care throughout all the changing scenes of life.

Questions

A personal journal exercise

> Guide me, O thou great Redeemer,
> Pilgrim through this barren land.

- Recall a time in your own life story when you have had to negotiate a significant transition.
- In retrospect, what was coming to an end?
- How did you experience the period of transition itself? What was most helpful for you? What was unhelpful?
- How did the transition become a turning point for something new?
- What did the experience teach you about the delicate work of accompanying others through transition?

For group discussion

- How well does your church support Christians at all ages and stages of faith?
- What are your own skills and preferences in the pastoral care of people at different periods of life?
- What sensitivities do you need to develop in order to accompany people through delicate points of transition?

---

7 See Further Reading.

Further Reading

Church of England, 1991, *How Faith Grows: Faith Development and Christian Education*, London: National Society/Church House Publishing.
Coles, Robert (ed.), 2000, *The Erik Erikson Reader*, New York: W. W. Norton and Company.
Fowler, James, 1987, *Faith Development and Pastoral Care*, Philadelphia: Fortress Press.
Gerkin, Charles V., 1997, *An Introduction to Pastoral Care*, Nashville: Abingdon.
Hagberg, Janet O. and Robert A. Guelich, 1995, *The Critical Journey: Stages in the Life of Faith*, Salem, WI: Sheffield Publishing Company.
Jamieson, Alan, 2002, *A Churchless Faith: Faith Journeys beyond Evangelical, Pentecostal and Charismatic Churches*, London: SPCK.
Kegan, Robert, 1982, *The Evolving Self: Problem and Process in Human Development*, Cambridge, MA: Harvard University Press.
Kelcourse, Felicity B. (ed.), 2004, *Human Development and Faith: Life-Cycle Stages of Body, Mind and Soul*, St Louis, MS: Chalice Press.
Loder, James E., 1998, *The Logic of the Spirit: Human Development in Theological Perspective*, San Francisco: Jossey-Bass.
Parks, Sharon and Robert Dykstra, 1986, *Faith Development and Fowler*, Birmingham, AL: Religious Education Press.
Watts, Fraser, Rebecca Nye and Sara Savage, 2002, *Psychology for Christian Ministry*, London: Routledge.

Introductory Reading on Particular Periods of the Life Cycle

Childhood

Nye, Rebecca, 2009, *Children's Spirituality: What It Is and Why It Matters*, London: Church House Publishing.
Richards, Anne and Peter Privett (eds), 2009, *Through the Eyes of a Child: New Insights in Theology from a Child's Perspective*, London: Church House Publishing.
Whithers, Margaret, 2006, *Mission-shaped Children: Moving Towards a Child-centred Church*, London: Church House Publishing.

Adolescence

Nash, Sally, 2011, *Youth Ministry: A Multi-Faceted Approach*, London: SPCK.
Vernon, Mark (ed.), 1997, *Pastoral Care for Young People*, London: MarshallPickering.
Ward, Pete, 1997, *Youthwork and the Mission of God*, London: SPCK.

Late adolescence

Daloz Parks, Sharon, 2000, *Big Questions, Worthy Dreams*, San Francisco: Jossey-Bass.
Graham, Alice, 'Identity in Middle and Late Adolescence', Chapter 10 in Kelcourse, Felicity B. (ed.), 2004, *Human Development and Faith: Life-Cycle Stage of Body, Mind and Soul*, St Louis, MS: Chalice Press.

Midlife

Kegan, Robert, 1982, *The Evolving Self: Problem and Process in Human Development*, Cambridge, MA: Harvard University Press.
Kidd, Sue Monk, 1990, *When the Heart Waits: Spiritual Direction for Life's Sacred Questions*, New York: HarperCollins.
Levinson, Daniel J., 1970, *The Stages of a Man's Life*, New York: Ballantine Books.
Rohr, Richard, 2011, *Falling Upward: A Spirituality for the Two Halves of Life*, San Francisco: John Wiley and Sons.

Old age

MacKinlay, Elizabeth, 2001, *The Spiritual Dimension of Ageing*, London: Jessica Kingsley.
Woodward, James, 2008, *Valuing Age: Pastoral Ministry with Older People*, London: SPCK.

4

All Desires Known

Sexuality and the Call of Love

Why should sex feature in a study guide on pastoral theology? Surely if we are serious about the call to fullness of life in Christ, then the sacred space of sexual desire is an area that cannot be ignored. Of course, that is not to say that theologians and pastors have not tried very hard over the centuries to deny the aching loveliness of sexuality in favour of a paler and passionless account of human flourishing! In this book, however, we insist that the whole of life is the arena of redemption. Not least in the profoundly integral area of sexuality, then, we must think very carefully about what that redemption might entail.

A Christian view of life has, we might say, a seriously ex-centric shape. That is to say that the centre of meaning, value and desire for a person of faith does not rest within herself but is outwardly directed in love towards its ultimate satisfaction in God. It was Augustine of Hippo who beautifully summed up the hope that fires each believing heart: 'You have made us for yourself, and our hearts are restless till they find their rest in you.'[1]

This perspective on human life and longing carries rich implications for pastoral care, as we attempt to reckon with the passionate forces of desire in human experience. If we believe that life in all its fullness is approached through a deep hunger and desire to know the surpassing love of God, then the way in which we nurture and respect our human stirrings of desire becomes a matter of crucial spiritual as well as developmental significance. In this chapter, we shall

---

1 *Confessions* I.1.

explore honestly some of the tensions and ambivalences in the ways in which desire – and especially sexual desire – has been portrayed within the Christian tradition, seeking to articulate a graceful discourse of desire which might foster a positive approach to contemporary pastoral care. From the outset, we shall need to affirm the rich significance of desire within the context of love.

Desire is love trying to happen

'Desire is love trying to happen', explains Sebastian Moore. 'It is the love that permeates the whole universe, trying to happen in me.'[2]

This is a good theological starting point as we try to make sense pastorally of the power of passions and desires amid the manifold complexities of human experience. For the purposes of this chapter, we shall take sexual desire as a paradigm for the many kinds of intense human yearnings which share something of the erotic quality of sexual passion. By focusing specifically on this paradigmatic sexual desire, we should be able to trace something of the developmental aspect of these natural longings, in a way which points towards the supremely pastoral goal of human maturity in Christ. Without naivety or oversimplification, we shall affirm that the gift of sexual desire is fundamental to the call of love. Desire can only be understood, in its fullest theological sense, as 'love trying to happen'.

This means that desire is an overwhelming gift of grace. The creative love that permeates the universe has blessed human beings with desires, which are both beautiful and outrageous. Moreover the Divine Lover, whom Christians know as the God and Father of Jesus Christ, is himself possessed of beautiful and outrageous desires, which reach out in passionate embrace towards the creatures that he has made. It is no wonder that saints and mystics down the ages have spoken of desire, yearning and longing as basic metaphors to describe their ardent search for the living God. This whole-souled and holy hunger for God, who is Love, is the fundamental passion which drives human beings towards that blissful union, now and eternally, for which they were created. And it is a passion whose mighty mysteries are most vividly portrayed by poetic souls.

---

2 Sebastian Moore, 2007, *Jesus the Liberator of Desire*, New York: Crossroad, p. 93.

Desire

For giving me desire,
An eager thirst, a burning ardent fire,
A virgin infant flame,
A love with which into the world I came,
An inward, hidden heavenly love,
Which in my soul did work and move,
And ever ever me inflame,
With restless longing heavenly avarice,
That never could be satisfied,
That did incessantly a Paradise
Unknown suggest, and something undescried
Discern, and bear me to it; be
Thy name for ever prais'd by me.

Thomas Traherne[3]

Yet, we find that there is something deeply ambivalent about the way in which desire has been regarded within the Christian tradition. Alongside a grudging recognition that all desires must find their source and fulfilment in God, the churches have more often peddled suspicions and primitive fears in the negative ways in which desire has been portrayed. Far from promoting a gracious discourse of desire, church teaching has often conspired to marginalize the passionate dimensions of human experience, concealing them beneath a dark veil of secrecy and shame. With such a problematic legacy of Christian attitudes towards sexuality and desire, it will be helpful for pastors to understand something of the complex history which has so embarrassingly coloured our contemporary perspectives.

---

3 From Bertram Dobell (ed.), 1932, *The Poetical Works of Thomas Traherne*, London, P. J. and A. E. Dobell, p. 76.

The long shadow of dualism

One of the most deep-rooted of all Christian heresies is the disvaluation of the body associated with dualistic beliefs. In contrast to the holistic appreciation of human creaturely life, which Christianity inherited from its Hebrew roots, a pervasive strain of dualistic Greek philosophy has infiltrated Christian thinking from its earliest days. This Neoplatonic tendency to regard matter as evil and reason or spirit as good, has recurred in many forms over the centuries – from the fourth-century Manichaean ethical dualism, which strongly influenced Augustine before his conversion, to the seventeenth-century Cartesian ontological dualism, which is so deeply entrenched in the rationalistic mindset of Western modernity.

Philosophers in the classical period taught that matter was inherently chaotic and that human nature could only ascend through the rule of rational will. This idea was developed through a widely used image of a chariot driven by a charioteer. Plato, for example, depicts the human struggle with chaotic forces through the extended metaphor of the charioteer who tries to steer two strong horses. One of the horses is white, representing the noble and spiritual impulses of life. The other horse is black, representing the base passions and crude instincts which drive human life towards destruction. Grappling with these opposing forces, Plato portrays the charioteer as the rational soul who must tame his unruly passions in the service of enlightened reason.

These archetypal themes – of bodily desires as wilful and chaotic and unbridled passions as leading to destruction – surface again and again in classic portrayals of the human psyche. It is reason which is acclaimed as the prime redemptive force, charged with taming the darker drives and instincts of the sinful flesh. It is interesting to note that there are traces of this primordial fear of forces not susceptible to reason even within the pages of the New Testament.

The apostolic writers, however, were at pains to challenge some of the prevailing dualism of their contemporaries. There is a particularly explicit rejection of dualism in the letter to the Colossians, for example, where the stringent asceticism promoted by Gnostic elements in the infant Church is refuted on the basis of the nature of God's redeeming initiative in Christ, in whom 'the whole fullness of deity dwells bodily' (Col. 2.9). Christian holiness, according to the apostle, is not furthered by drastic discipline and iron-willed mortification of fleshly appetites, but rather through faithful identification with the incarnate, crucified and risen Christ, who calls all people to be renewed in the image of their Creator (Col. 3.10).

It is against this robustly Christological background that we should read other New Testament passages which warn against the moral dangers of 'the desires of the flesh'. Careful New Testament scholarship reveals that the opposition of flesh (*sarx*) and spirit (*pneuma*) should not be interpreted in crudely dualistic terms as a conflict between the unruly sexual desires of the body and the pure spiritual desires of the rational soul. A closer reading of the epistles shows that even when Paul is at his most vehement in condemning life 'in the flesh' his accusations are targeted against a whole panoply of disordered affections and behaviours which oppose the life of the spirit. He is equally concerned, for example, to expose the destructive nature of self-righteousness or jealousy (1 Cor. 3.3; Gal. 3.2–3; Phil. 3.3–4), as to inveigh against the carnal excesses of sexual lust (Gal. 5.16–21).

We can summarize the hopeful message of the New Testament by rejoicing that, in and through Jesus' fullness of life, we are promised not the eradication of desire, but rather the liberation of desire towards its true goal of divine love.

Despite this glorious good news, however, the young Church still struggled to break free from the dualistic climate of Greek thought. Throughout the early centuries, perennial forms of Christian dualism persisted in the moral anxiety that the body was inherently problematic, its sinful carnalities needing to be taken firmly in hand by reason and will, assisted to greater or lesser extent by the help of God the Holy Spirit.

It was this kind of disparagement of the body and its passions which coloured the imagination of Augustine through his early exposure to Manichaean teaching. We need to remember that, like the apostle Paul, Augustine is a complex figure, who should not bear all the blame for the tragic incoherence of later Christian theology and practice. It is clear, for example, that he rejects the cosmic dualism of the Manichees, which undermines the goodness of creation and rules out the full intercourse of flesh and spirit in the incarnation. Nevertheless, we cannot deny the overwhelmingly negative portrayal of sexual desire which permeates Augustine's writing and which has so heavily influenced all subsequent Christian doctrine. His personal struggles with sexual continence, exposed in florid detail through the tortured account of the *Confessions*, reflect such a painfully distorted experience of bodily passions that Augustine can sustain no distinction between wholesome, natural desire and evil, lustful concupiscence. Pursuing a similar rationale, his reading of Genesis led to a fateful equation of original sin with sexual activity which is nowhere supported within the biblical text itself.

In the face of this crushingly negative inherited tradition, it is important for us to reassert, with Sebastian Moore, that desire itself is *not* sin but rather 'love wanting to happen'.[4] Our brief historic review of the dualistic influences on Christian thought and culture has shown how deep-seated are the primitive fears which drive a wedge of suspicion between godliness and sexual passion, and how vital, therefore, is the need for a graceful and authentically Christian discourse of desire. For some pointers towards a more constructive theology of desire, we shall turn next to the poetic wisdom of the mystics.

The mystic vision

Human beings are fundamentally 'wired' for love: and this is part of our creaturely glory. Our deepest erotic desires, which drive us to reach out to others, are implanted in our created nature to orient us towards all that is good and life-giving. What is more, these desires, with all their energy and urgency for good or for ill, represent a vital powerhouse of human spirituality. This is the poetic insight of the mystics, men and women in every generation who have expressed their burning desire for God in terms that are never less than passionate, full-bodied and sometimes audaciously sensuous.

> ### The flame of divine love
>
> Our Lord said: 'I longed for you before the beginning of the world. I long for you and you long for me. Where two burning desires meet, there love is made perfect.'
>
> Mechthild of Magdeburg[5]

---

4 Sebastian Moore, 2007, *The Contagion of Jesus: Doing Theology as if it Mattered*, London: Darton, Longman and Todd, p. 105.

5 Mechthild of Magdeburg, 1988, *The Flowing Light of the Godhead*, transl. F. Tobin, New York: Paulist Press, VII.16.

We find an especially thought-provoking discussion of mystical theology in the writing of one of Augustine's near-contemporaries, Gregory of Nyssa. In his late fourth-century treatise on the spirituality of celibates and married people, Gregory adopts the imagery of desire as a forceful stream which, rightly directed, leads the soul to God. According to Gregory, the cultivation and discipline of desire is central to a spiritually productive life, being richly irrigated through the softening, fructifying stirrings of the soul. Far from suppressing the passions, Gregory is concerned to deepen and direct them towards their true goal in God. Surprisingly he finds marriage, for this purpose, to furnish as excellent a training ground as monastic celibacy. The point is that a seriously attentive chastening, renewing, transforming and intensifying of the passions, in whatever state of human sexual relationships, will nourish an abundance of the fruit of the Spirit, which flowers supremely in love.

In this vision, Gregory is entirely faithful to the scriptures which freely use sexual imagery to describe the ardent love that flows between God and his creatures (for example in the Song of Solomon) and between Christ and his Church (cf. Eph. 5.25–32). Interestingly, he also foreshadows some of the remarkable teaching of spiritual writers from Julian of Norwich to Ignatius Loyola who are not shy of using the most intimate language of desire to express their thirst for God. Central to the wisdom of these mystics is the exercise of a wise discernment which distinguishes healthy desires from unhealthy and destructive obsessions. As with Gregory, it is through the education and right direction, rather than the eradication and suppression of desire, that true spiritual growth can be encouraged and sustained.

All these lovers of God learned from experience that the most dangerous struggles and tensions of desire arise from a false and addictive preoccupation with the self. It is not the forcefulness of passion which is corrupting to the spiritual life, but rather its misdirection, its deadly turning inward towards a distorted self-gratification, which exchanges the attractiveness of God for the false allure of idols. These are the degrading passions that must be baptized into Christ if they are to find their freedom in the grace and power of his Holy Spirit. In the last analysis, the problem with desire is not the unbridled body, but the feckless soul which craves for ultimacy in a goal which is less than God.

A desiring God

Lurking behind Christianity's lingering suspicions about human desire there remains an idealized image of a passionless God. This kind of Olympian godhead, who is blissfully self-contained, unperturbed and at rest, should never be affected by the yearning and vulnerability so familiar to turbulent humanity. Such a classic doctrine of divine impassibility, however, in its concern to preserve the incomparability of God's perfections, comes perilously close to evacuating God's love of any meaningful redemptive power.

Christian trinitarian theology, by contrast, challenges such aloof notions of impassive perfection, rejoicing in a God whose boundless self-giving is vibrant with passion and desire, vulnerability and eros. Christians worship this God-in-loving-Trinity whose passion sustains an eternal dynamic of desire at the very heart of the universe. And human beings themselves are caught up in this passionate exchange: 'the whole story of creation, incarnation and our incorporation into the fellowship of Christ's body tells us that God desires us'.[6]

> ### The Annunciation
>
> Now in this iron reign
> I sing the liberty
> Where each asks from each
> What each most wants to give
> And each awakes in each
> What else would never be,
> Summoning so the rare
> Spirit to breathe and live.
>
> Then let us empty out
> Our hearts until we find
> The last least trifling toy,
> Since now all turns to gold,

---

6 Rowan Williams, 2002, 'The Body's Grace', in *Theology and Sexuality: Classic and Contemporary Readings*, edited by E. F. Rogers (Jnr), Malden, MA: Blackwell, p. 311.

> And everything we have
> Is wealth of heart and mind,
> That squandered thus in turn
> Grows with us manifold.
>
> Giving, I'd give you next
> Some more than mortal grace,
> But that you deifying
> Myself I might deify,
> Forgetting love was born
> Here in a time and place,
> And robbing by such praise
> This life we magnify.
>
> Whether the soul at first
> This pilgrimage began,
> Or the shy body leading
> Conducted soul to soul
> Who knows? This is the most
> That soul and body can,
> To make us each for each
> And in our spirit whole.
>
> Edwin Muir (1887–1959)[7]

It is in the image of this desiring God that Christians are called towards a maturity of love. The astonishing story of God's incarnation, with all its risky, kenotic and vulnerable self-involvement, presents to us the Word made Flesh as the ultimate locus for the redemption of our bodies. It is this transcending love, which beckons us to a similar abandonment, in a responsive desire, which calls out the fullest investment of heart, soul and bodily adoration. Embraced by a crucified love, human beings find liberation from the death-dealing forces of obsession, to seek the true consummation of self-giving through relationships of eager and reciprocal desire.

---

7 Edwin Muir, 1960, *Collected Poems*, London: Faber & Faber, p. 117.

The call of love

We have seen that there are sound theological reasons to revise some of the negative disvaluations of sexual passion in the historic tradition and thence to approach the 'education of desire' as a potential royal road towards the goal of Christian maturity in love.[8]

Picking up the pastoral agenda that was laid out in the last chapter, we might now reflect a little further on some of the opportunities and challenges for pastoral care which arise in the course of human sexual development through the life cycle. Desire is deeply rooted in human biological dynamics: we are, in other words, 'wired' for love. Since we observe, both from everyday experience and from the expanding field of research in psychology and the human sciences, that the processes of sexual maturation are attended by far-reaching changes in human identity and relationships through the whole course of life, then we must recognize a pastoral imperative to consider how the 'education of desire' might be encouraged at key points of human growth and transition.

This is a delicate agenda, since there is no doubt that human desires can be experienced in ways which are both complex and difficult to direct. It would be dangerously naive for pastors to underestimate the force of their insistent urging. But it would be equally unhelpful for Christians to deny the inherent goodness of physical, emotional and spiritual instincts which exist to lead us out of ourselves and into the arms of others. Let us consider then, first, how these instincts can be shaped towards maturity in the unfolding dynamics of the life cycle. We shall then be in a clearer position to reflect on how the various corruptions of desire might be robustly addressed.

Learning love and letting go

Some of the most sensitive insights of psychological studies relate to the ways in which human erotic desire comes to be shaped and transformed through the experiences of life. We saw in the last chapter how developmental theories of various kinds inform a pastoral vision of maturity in Christ. It is worth reflecting in more detail on the extent to which the sexual dynamics operating at

---

8 Timothy Gorringe, 2000, *The Education of Desire*, London: SCM.

different points of the life cycle may either contribute to, or alternatively confound, that growing maturity and wholeness.

Psychologists from Freud onwards have alerted us to the power of the most primitive attachments which play out in the course of human life, from the first hungry cries of infancy onward. Our earliest experiences of desire – intense, inchoate and pre-verbal – are fraught with intimations of acute vulnerability and need. The child's craving for the mother's breast is the most elemental passion which patterns and prefigures all subsequent experiences of human desire.

Yet, we know that no human parent will fully satisfy every hunger of her growing child. While Donald Winnicott has helpfully identified the profound emotional value of 'good-enough' mothering,[9] holding and responding to the needs of the infant with sufficiently faithful devotion to lay the foundations of all subsequent trusting relationships, we recognize nonetheless a certain insatiable quality in all human desires. However 'good enough' a generous parental response to infantile need may be, the inherent boundlessness of desire and the aching limitations which qualify all biological attachments leave the human soul yearning for ultimate satisfaction in the arms of God (Ps. 131.2).

Yet, throughout the course of life it seems to be that these 'good enough' reflections of the divine image, which are found within all faithful relationships, can furnish a 'rich enough' soil for godly desire to take root. It is precisely within our primal experiences of desire-as-need, which is in no sense sinful in itself, that human beings begin to be educated towards that mature capacity for intimacy and reciprocal tenderness, which flowers when desire is fully transformed by love. The human Christ himself experienced the hunger of desire-as-need throughout his life, from his infant dependence on his mother to his adult desire for the care and closeness of human companions (Matt. 26.38), culminating in his profound capacity to let go into the loving arms of his Father (Luke 23.46).

Further along the road of human development, each unfolding stage of sexual maturation will present fresh opportunities to open up to the call of love. Leaving childhood behind, for example, the rapid changes of adolescence propel young people beyond their inner loneliness to an eager reaching out for intimacy. The first adolescent experiences of sexual arousal and genital pleasure may be as bewildering as they are exciting – not only for young people trying to make sense of their deepening desires, but also for those adults privileged to

---

9 Donald Winnicott, 'Transitional objects and transitional phenomena; a study of the first not-me possession', *International Journal of Psychoanalysis*, 1953; 34(2), pp. 89–97.

> **Te Deum**
>
> You are the source of our yearning, O Christ:
> you are the way of glory.
> Bearing our sweet and humble flesh,
> fruit of a woman's womb,
> you were made and moulded as we are
> by human particular touch.
>
> Janet Morley[10]

accompany them through inevitable periods of awkwardness, questioning and experimentation. Amid these far-reaching changes and challenges, the grace and stability of a Christian community which is willing to support and affirm young people can be an outstandingly valuable pastoral resource.

The progression towards adulthood invites a movement towards mature mutuality and intimacy, which is one of the richest fruits of Christian marriage. Couples are called to open themselves up to one another in love, discovering how in their own bodies they can give and receive pleasure; and learning, especially through the delights and demands of family life, more of that radical ex-centricity which harvests the fruits of love in order that they may be shared.

But the ideal of mutual love which is embraced in the normative pattern of heterosexual family life should not be exalted in ways which deny the rich complexities of human sexual nature. It is arguably the begrudging shallowness of the churches' inherited theology of desire which has led to a prim and sadly evasive treatment of adult sexual aspirations which flower in alternative contexts – often with devastating pastoral results.

Two groups of young adults in particular have suffered from a lack of candour among Christian communities about the real challenges of pursuing an ideal, lifelong and faithful relationship. In the first place, many single women have been profoundly ill-served by churches which promote high expectations of (female) chastity in a demographic where the number of potential (Christian) partners is heavily biased in favour of eligible males. Second, and more fiercely debated, is the continuing fearful uncertainty in the churches about the theological value which should be ascribed to loving same-sex partnerships.

It is not the prime concern of this book to try to resolve ethical debates about

---

10 Janet Morley, 1992, *All Desires Known*, London: SPCK, p. 33.

homosexuality, which have threatened the unity of Christians more than any other issue in recent years.[11] What is vital for pastors is an honest commitment to the education of desire, in whatever context of vulnerable mutuality such desire may be awakened. For some ministers this will entail a costly personal and public reworking of their own inherited frameworks of sexual ethical behaviour. This is a pastoral necessity; since anyone who is trusted to share with others in their deepest dreams and desires for love must forge a pastoral integrity which is never less than truthful and always full of hope for the redemptive possibilities of covenanted love.

Later on in life, beyond the intensely formative years of adolescence and young adulthood, the call of love continues to beckon. For many people, it can be the transitions of older life which prompt a deeper reflection on the dynamics of intimacy, as diminishing sexual capacity and the accumulated challenges of personal loss present increasing opportunities to give love away – with decreasing prospects of any self-gratifying return. Pastoral sensitivity to the loneliness of older people becomes an especial challenge in an aging society, and one which merits deeper theological reflection on the invitation to grow in grace through physical diminishment.

> **No, no, there is no going back**
>
> Less and less you are
> that possibility you were.
> More and more you have become
> those lives and deaths
> that have belonged to you.
> You have become a sort of grave
> containing much that was
> and is no more in time, beloved ...
> ... Every day you have less reason
>   not to give yourself away.
>
> Wendell Berry[12]

---

11 For a helpful introduction to this debate from the perspective of the Anglican Communion, see Philip Groves (ed.), 2008, *The Anglican Communion and Homosexuality*, London: SPCK.

12 Wendell Berry, 1998, *A Timbered Choir: The Sabbath Poems 1979–1997*, new edition, York: Counterpoint, p. 167.

There is more about love to be learned at every stage of life. The pastoral vision of educating desire towards maturity bears rich fruit through a progressive ascetic transformation of self-seeking passions, in order that human beings might learn to entrust themselves towards a finally self-less 'letting go' into the welcoming arms of God.

The corruption of desire

Pastoral theology begins and ends in grace: and the gracious gift of mutual love is fundamental to a redemptive approach to human desiring. But there is also a shadow side to human desire which, when turned in on the self, works against the loving ex-centricity to which we are invited in the image of God. We have seen how, too often in traditional theological reflection, the darker side of sexuality has been simplistically equated with the sub-rational instinctive passions, with the result that wholesome sexual appetites have been repressed and false asceticisms have bred all kinds of unholy corruption.

A more gracious appraisal of human desire dare not be naive, however, about the tragic seriousness of temptations to sin. This is evident, for example, in the way that churches have recently had to address urgent questions in the area of sexual behaviour through their extensive work on safeguarding. We shall consider some of the practical issues relating to the disciplined management of intimate relationships in a later chapter (see Chapter 9 on Boundaries and Power), but at this stage it is important to reflect more carefully on some of the sources of sinful corruption which work to distort and derail one of the most precious aspects of our God-given human nature.

Exploitation and abuse, violence and lustful greed, are arguably the most flagrant manifestations of the perverted passions, which refuse the outward call of love, turning human beings instead to an inwardly directed passion, which seeks gratification in and for the egotistic self. Yet, while it is easy to identify some of the more pastorally destructive outworkings of sexual corruption in individual behaviour, it can be harder to recognize the pervasive influence of social and cultural forces which work subtly to undermine the redemptive potential of human sexual fulfilment in a whole society.

Economic forces in particular can be highly pernicious in the ways that they operate to degrade contemporary images of sexual desire. In the modern Western world, sexual desire is artificially stimulated through a profoundly corrupted advertising milieu, which promotes an erotically charged agenda within popular music, fashion and consumer markets. For young men and women in particular, the insidious effect of everyday immersion in this culture is 'the temptation to internalize, to slide uncritically into, and to adopt the roles of sex marauder and sex object respectively'.[13]

The unmasking of such predatory forces is equally important within the Christian community as it is within the wider economy; and it is partly for this reason that pastoral workers need to be critically aware of their own motivations and potential for self-gratification. Later chapters will examine how the deep and rich projections of spiritual desire can focus, more or less helpfully, on individual representative ministers. But at this point it should be sufficient to note that the misuse of religious power, and the manipulation by authority figures of secrecy and shame, can be every bit as corrosive to genuine desire as, for example, the misuse of the secular media through pornography.

There is a destructive aspect to human passions which Christians have traditionally discussed in terms of the 'deadly sins', notably pride, gluttony and lust. An enlightened and gracious understanding of our sexual nature will help us to overcome the dangers of unrestrained and self-serving passion: not through fear and repression, but through an expectant confidence in the creative and redemptive purposes of God.

A Prayer for Purity

Almighty God
to whom all hearts are open,
all desires known,
and from whom no secrets are hidden:
cleanse the thoughts of our hearts
by the inspiration of your Holy Spirit,
that we may perfectly love you,
and worthily magnify your holy name;
through Christ our Lord.

Anglican Eucharistic collect

---

13 Adrian Thatcher, 2011, *God, Sex and Gender: An Introduction*, Oxford: Wiley-Blackwell, p. 200.

Redeeming desire

Beyond the shallowness and cynicism of much of our public cheapening of desire and beyond the prim evasiveness that has sadly typified many traditional Christian reactions, there lies a beckoning tract of thought and language which is reverent, hopeful and radiant with redemptive beauty. This is the gracious ground of holy desiring, which pastors are called to evoke with tenderness and joy.

We have argued in this chapter for the rearticulation of a gracious discourse of desire. In the present climate of church debate and the unseemly culture of much of our wider society, it has never been more necessary for pastors to seek out new redemptive paths of reflection, communication and care.

One way in which the Church invites all Christians to taste the fullness of desire is through the sacrament of the Eucharist, the occasion which Adrian Thatcher is bold enough to call 'God's way of making love'.[14] Though some may find his analogy a little too direct, it points to the gloriously tangible reality of souls being drawn, through desire, into an experience of deep abandonment to a love that is wholly and eternally faithful. This is the vision of a theologically and pastorally holistic imagination – confident in the trust that deep calls to deep in the enactment of Christ's utter self-giving, which is bodily surrendered for the redemption and satisfaction of all human yearning.

Infusing passion with reverence and enfolding reverence within holy desire, good pastoral care will embody a gracious and disciplined vision of human sexuality, which is being humbly purified and artfully matured in response to the endlessly inviting love of God.

Questions

- In your own experience of the church's pastoral care, how has human sexuality been affirmed and blessed?
- In your own experience of the church's pastoral care, how has the expression of desire been repressed or marginalized?

---

14 Thatcher, *God, Sex and Gender*, p. 110.

- How do you respond to the language of desire when it is expressed in a religious context – for example in the Song of Solomon, in the prayers of the mystics, or in contemporary worship songs?
- What do you notice about the role models which the Church projects – in its advertising, for example, or in those who are looked up to in leadership? What kind of images of sexuality do they portray?
- As you reflect on your own calling to pastoral ministry, how do you seek to express and embody a gracious discourse of desire?

Further Reading

Atwell, Robert (ed.), 2005, *Love: 100 Readings in Celebration of Marriage and Love*, Norwich: Canterbury Press.

Coakley, Sarah, 2012, *The New Asceticism: Sexuality, Gender and the Quest for God*, London: Continuum.

Gorringe, Timothy J., 2000, *The Education of Desire*, London: SCM.

Ind, Jo. 2003, *Memories of Bliss: God, Sex and Us*, London: SCM Press.

Moore, Sebastian, 2007, *Jesus the Liberator of Desire*, New York: Crossroad.

Roberts, Robert C., 2007, *Spiritual Emotions: A Psychology of Christian Virtues*, Grand Rapids: Eerdmans.

Sheldrake, Philip, 2001, *Befriending our Desires*, London: Darton, Longman and Todd.

Shults, F. LeRon and Jan-Olav Henrikson (eds), 2011, *Saving Desire: The Seduction of Christian Theology*, Grand Rapids: Eerdmans.

Thatcher, Adrian, 2011, *God, Sex and Gender: An Introduction*, Oxford: Wiley-Blackwell.

Williams, Rowan, 2002, 'The Body's Grace', in *Theology and Sexuality: Classic and Contemporary Readings*, edited by E. F. Rogers (Jnr), Malden, MA: Blackwell.

5

The Fragility of Life
Attachment, Trauma and Loss

The joys of love and the pains of grief both touch the essence of what it means to be human. For pastors who are learning what it means to care, few things could be more important than to reckon with these two perennially mysterious aspects of human experience. In this chapter, we shall turn our thoughts to the tragic dimensions of human frailty and finitude, searching out what kind of theological resources might enable a ministry of healing. Our focus will be on the immensely tender encounters with suffering, grief and loss which cry out for pastoral kindness and wisdom.

Christian churches still offer, in a host of different ways, a ministry of pastoral care and support to countless individuals and families, particularly at times of loss. This ministry of prayer and presence is typically quiet, undemonstrative and easily taken for granted. Yet, it is notable that, despite a widespread loss of regular contact with religious teaching and practice, many people in our secularized society still turn instinctively to the Church to seek help and consolation at times of major tragedy and grief. Whether wistful half-believers or people of strong faith, those going through the deep waters of suffering and bereavement long for the comfort and reassurance of a hope that is anchored in God.

This chapter will introduce some of the essential foundations for a faithful Christian ministry to the suffering, dying and the bereaved, tracing the landscape of loss in all its exquisite sensitivity and sketching a tentative pastoral vision for compassionate care and support.

THE FRAGILITY OF LIFE

Frailty and finitude

Part of life's mystery is its terrible fragility. Despite our best human efforts to protect ourselves and those we love, the changes and chances of earthly life promise no lasting stability and no certainty or assurance that any of us will be immune from affliction. Religious wisdom teaches, on the contrary, that all human life is vulnerable to sorrow and sadness and that true faith is not a matter of denying fragility, but rather of seeking the resources to grow through it.

The scriptures often picture human vulnerability before God in terms of the ultimate dependence of a child. 'Frail children of dust, and feeble as frail, in Thee do we trust, nor find Thee to fail', as the familiar hymn renders the psalmist's cry (Ps. 104.27–30). This is not to indulge an infantilized response to common human frailty, but to promote a realistic and trustful sense of dependence on God.

It is easy to lose sight of this ineluctable vulnerability in a culture which has become fixated with the avoidance of risk. Modern Western societies, with all the benefits of insurance, social security and generous health provision, do their level best to cushion individuals from the existential impact of frailty and finitude – until tragedy comes finally and fearfully close to home. At such times, the shock of facing up to the realities of human affliction is then all the harder to bear.

> As a father has compassion on his children,
> so is the Lord merciful towards those who fear him.
> For he knows of what we are made;
> he remembers that we are but dust.
> Our days are but as grass;
> we flourish as a flower of the field;
> For as soon as the wind blows over it, it is gone,
> and its place shall know it no more.
> But the merciful goodness of the Lord is from of old
> and endures for ever on those who fear him,
> and his righteousness on children's children.
>
> Psalm 103.13–17

Historians and social anthropologists describe stark contrasts in modern attitudes to death in comparison to our forebears. The demography of bereavement has changed beyond recognition in recent centuries. From the days when death could strike at random in any village or any family, making the experience of bereavement utterly commonplace and natural, modern societies with less routine experience of the intrusion of tragedy have fostered an illusion that death can somehow be kept under control, or for the most part held at bay.

One worrying result of changing life expectancy is that the encounter with death has become unfamiliar and remote, so that our shared cultural resources for responding to it are correspondingly less secure. Whereas an earlier Christian culture sought to enfold its members in an art of dying (*ars moriendi*) as much as in a shared understanding of living, the ways of approaching death and bereavement in our post-modern society have now fragmented to become a matter of personal choice. The ongoing debate about legalization of assisted dying is one very telling example of this breakdown of shared social values.

In such a context, Christian pastors need to reflect deeply on the rich resources of our theological and liturgical traditions, considering how best to make these available to those who may seek our care. It will be beyond the scope of this book to explore in detail the range of ministries appropriate to prayerful healing or the enormous contribution of Christian funeral ministry; but the broad principles of theological, psychological and pastoral responses to suffering and loss are laid out in this chapter so as to provide an essential orientation for any pastoral worker who is beginning to make a contribution in this area.

An unfailing covenant

For people of faith it is clear that neither the protection afforded by socio-economic security, nor the promise of ever-improving medical technology, can finally assuage our primitive existential fear of mortality. Although we should rejoice that many of the fearsome causes of death and dependence can be deferred through the blessings of modern health and social care, we must also recognize that frailty and finitude continue as inalienable aspects of human nature which cry out for deeper, spiritual resources of wisdom and care.

We have seen in Chapter 2 (Being Human) that a Christian vision of life in all its fullness is one which is not diminished by the realities of suffering and death. On the contrary, a theological anthropology which images human beings in relationship with the eternal life and love of the Trinity directs us towards an unfailing spring of hope and consolation in the face of heartbreak and loss.

We can find many entry points within the scriptures for pastoral reflection on suffering and loss. Traditionally Christians have often turned to the Hebrew psalms with their poignant evocations of the many shades of human experience. The psalms show us how to give voice to lament, uttering deep outpourings of anguish and questioning alongside heartfelt shouts of thanksgiving and praise. This powerful tension between dreadful anguish and fervent faith is held together within a typically forthright expression of soulful prayer.

> How long, O Lord? Will you forget me forever?
> How long will you hide your face from me?
> How long must I bear pain in my soul,
> and have sorrow in my heart all day long?
> How long shall my enemy be exalted over me?
> … But I trusted in your steadfast love;
> my heart shall rejoice in your salvation.
> I will sing to the Lord,
> because he has dealt bountifully with me. (Ps. 13.1–2, 5–6)

In a different genre, the prophetic writers also plumb the depths of human distress as they grapple theologically with the appalling disorientation visited upon the people through political catastrophes, humiliation and exile. Again and again, the prophets return to the theme of God's faithful covenant and the unbreakable bond of care which God has established with the people who are called by his name.

> But Zion said, "The Lord has forsaken me,
> my Lord has forgotten me."
> Can a woman forget her nursing child,
> or show no compassion for the child of her womb?
> Even these may forget,
> yet I will not forget you.
> See, I have inscribed you on the palms of my hands. (Isa. 49.14–16)

Christians read these powerful testimonies from the Hebrew scriptures through the lens of Jesus' own cross and resurrection and the promise of inexhaustible comfort which he bequeaths to the Church.

> Blessed be the God and Father of our Lord Jesus Christ,
> the Father of all mercies and the God of all consolation,
> who consoles us in all our affliction,
> so that we are able to console those who are in any affliction
> with the consolation with which we ourselves
> are consoled by God. (2 Cor. 1.3–4)

However, it would be foolish to imagine that we can nail down any text or trite theological formulation, Christian or otherwise, which pastors can turn to in order to neatly 'answer' the searing questions posed by human suffering. What the scriptures point towards, and what saints throughout the generations have borne witness to, is a powerful experience of the mysterious, unbreakable bond of God's loving faithfulness, which richly sustains the agonized soul. And because this bond has been sealed in the deepest and costliest sacrifice, through the shedding of Christ's own blood, there is no human loss, no crisis, no trial or tribulation which can ever exhaust his promise.

> For I am convinced that neither death nor life,
> ... nor anything else in all creation,
> will be able to separate us from the love of God
> in Christ Jesus our Lord. (Rom. 8.38–39).

Attachment and security

An abiding sense of deep and unbreakable bonds of attachment is one of the most precious anchors for any human being in times of trouble. Modern psychological understandings of the emotional significance of personal 'attachment' provide many fruitful insights for a contemporary understanding of the dynamics of suffering and loss. In the light of this theoretical resource, Christian thinkers are increasingly reflecting on the concept of 'attachment' as a richly suggestive model for thinking about the pastoral dimensions of our human relationship with God.[1]

Current thinking about attachment theory has its roots in comparisons between animal behaviour research (ethology) and psychoanalytic studies of children. In the framework developed by John Bowlby, the concept of 'attachment' is used to describe a close affectional bond typically developing between a young infant and her parent. Bowlby recognized that a secure sense of attachment at a young age is fostered by warmth and affection, sensitivity, responsiveness and constancy, and that children who are deprived of these foundational experiences of parental attachment may struggle to develop trusting intimate relationships in future life.

The characteristics of a good attachment relationship were outlined by Mary Ainsworth's studies of parenting behaviour.

- Safe haven – when the child feels threatened or afraid, she can return to the caregiver for comfort and protection.
- Secure base – the caregiver offers a secure and dependable base from which to go out confidently and explore the world.
- Proximity maintenance – the child strives to stay close to the caregiver, whom she trusts will keep her from harm.
- Separation distress – when separated from the caregiver, the child will express anxiety and distress.

Building on these original insights, a wealth of psychological theory and application has unfolded as the dynamics of attachment behaviour have been closely examined at every stage of life. From the earliest stages of elemental trust described by Erikson through to the devastating trauma of grief when intense bonds of relationship are severed, attachment theory can illuminate the way in which close ties of durable human commitment are foundational for emotional security and well-being.

It is perhaps not surprising, then, that similar patterns of trust, dependence and constancy can be discerned in the way that believers try to describe a personal relationship with God. Although it can be misleading to press the analogies too far, there are profound connections to be drawn between the experiences of

---

1 See for example Lee A. Kirkpatrick, 2005, *Attachment, Evolution, and the Psychology of Religion*, New York: Guildford Press.

human intimacy and the security that comes from a trustful relationship with God. Since human language about God and our ways of conceiving his presence can only be expressed in terms we can understand, it is entirely natural that we should think and speak of loving and nurturing relationships as a kind of spiritual attachment to an infinitely caring God. It is from such deep wells of consoling spirituality that pastors learn to draw their resources as they come alongside people in suffering.

- God is a safe haven: *When I am afraid, I put my trust in you* (Ps. 56.3).
- God is a secure base: *You are indeed my rock and my fortress; for your name's sake lead me and guide me* (Ps. 31.3).
- Proximity maintenance is a spiritual necessity: *Your face, Lord, do I seek. Do not hide your face from me* (Ps. 27.8–9).
- Separation distress drives the yearning soul back to God: *Do not forsake me, O Lord; O my God, do not be far from me; make haste to help me, O Lord, my salvation* (Ps. 38.21–22).

Establishing and sustaining a strong relationship of attachment to God can be seen in this light as one of the focal priorities for Christian maturity. In the remainder of this chapter we shall explore how this priority might be addressed in situations of crisis, and specifically in ministry to the sick, the dying and the bereaved.

Crisis and disorientation

How are we to imagine a faithful Christian response to sorrow and grief, when the most vital attachments of earthly life are mortally threatened? We began to sketch out in Chapter 3 (Faithful Change) how the crises of life, whether developmental or situational, furnish both challenges and opportunities for a deeper spiritual maturity. Such crises can be particularly acute at times of loss when all the familiar landmarks of emotional security are grievously disturbed.

Of course, the crisis of bereavement is not the only kind of painful upheaval to assail the human spirit. Profound disorientation can result from any major life event – the loss of a job, break up of a marriage, a financial crisis, an accident or illness, an unwanted pregnancy, a major move of home or occupation, a local or national disaster, the challenge of caring for elderly parents, the birth of a disabled child. In any of these situational crises, the whole architecture of emotional and spiritual security can be shaken to the core as the taken-for-granted landscape of familiar attachments is drastically unsettled.

To generalize about the experience of loss, however, can be patronizing at best and, at worst, cruelly off target. It is sadly neither true nor helpful to say to anyone, 'I know how you feel'. If we draw any wisdom from scientific theories of the common human experience of grief, we would be wiser still to remember that loss is so exquisitely painful largely because it is so uniquely individual. There are nevertheless sufficient basic commonalities in the broad movements of loss and readaptation which, sensitively considered, can help to inform a tentative pastoral response.

Figure 5.1 The U curve of loss

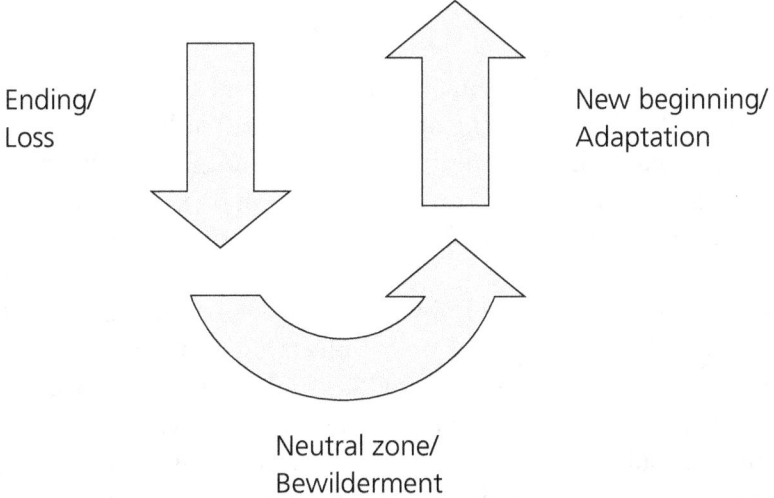

The simple U curve of transition which was introduced in Chapter 3 is a helpful reminder of the depth of dissonance and disorientation which accompanies grief. Whether long drawn out, or desperately acute, the experience of plunging down into a deep valley of anxious bewilderment is something which most of us recognize only too well. It is into this territory that the pastor brings a Christian presence.

The first prerequisite in ministering to someone in the depths of anguish is presence. It is not to offer a sophisticated theoretical explanation of their situation, but simply and genuinely to show that you care. How that care is expressed in practice may be an awkward combination of the love of the amateur and the discernment of the professional. But the humble pastor strives to bring a professional steadiness in the midst of crisis together with all the tender-heartedness of the sincere friend, aware that in the midst of sorrow she too is a frail earthen vessel whose strength and consolation comes only from God (2 Cor.4.7).

It is the rock-like character of that strength and consolation, founded on God, which can be a vital gift to share in a crisis. While many people show enormous resilience in the face of suffering and loss, there are times of overwhelming distress in the lives of many individuals and families when the need for an upholding presence is acute and raw. At such times, the steady objectivity as well as the loving sensitivity of the minister will be crucial.

Pastoral Story

Martin, the 24-year-old son of a somewhat disaffected church family, was tragically killed in a climbing accident. Several of his friends had shared connections with the church as boys – through the church school and scouts group or as bell ringers. His fiancée lived 70 miles away. His parents and younger brother and sister suffered intense shock.

The vicar's first contact with Martin's parents was delicate, but purposeful. He established clear and open communication with the family and made prompt arrangements for the timing of the funeral. He briefed key members of the pastoral team and paid a visit to the pub and the local school, where Martin was still fondly remembered. Prayers were said in church every day, and several local friends called in to light candles. The vicar made time for visits as well as phone calls and emails, as details of the funeral began to take shape. There were many moments of deep, tender silence, as the dreadful shock was held and shared. And there were gentle smiles, as well as tears, as bitter-sweet stories from Martin's childhood were passed around members of the gathered family.

> The funeral was a memorable occasion, with a fabulous peal of bells as Martin's coffin was taken out of church. A year later, when Martin's former fiancée visited the church on the anniversary of his death, she called to thank the vicar for the care that the church had shown. She had never realized how much the support of a Christian community could mean and was now attending a church in her own area, where she hoped to be confirmed.

A simple model of practical crisis intervention can be adapted for pastors who are drawn in to help people at times of overwhelming distress. Switzer and Stone offer an outline of the 'ABC' of pastoral crisis counselling which goes some way to shaping the generic dynamics of effective crisis support.[2]

A – Achieve contact. When people are deeply shocked or troubled, the initial approach is a sensitive matter. The arrival of a church minister, with or without a dog collar, may not be an immediate source of reassurance to some people; and care must be taken to achieve and to build rapport. The skills of attentive listening are essential, offering a full and undivided attention together with deep and generous empathy.

B – Boil down the problem to its essentials. It is easy to be ineffective in a crisis, when the intensity of feelings tumble out in infantile distress, or threaten to paralyze otherwise normally competent adults. The pastor, similarly, may feel deeply unsettled by a shocking situation and find it hard to focus on what can be done to help. It takes a cool head and a warm heart to attend deeply to the issues at hand, offering sufficient meaningful response – whether emotional, spiritual or utterly practical – to ease the burden of immediate distress and bring the assurance of ongoing support.

C – Cope actively with the situation. The beginnings of a turn towards adaptation lie in the ability to look purposefully towards the future. Beyond mere sympathy, the sensitive pastor can help to facilitate an intentional response to a crisis by helping people to mobilize their spiritual, emotional and practical resources for the next steps that must be taken.

---

2 David Switzer, 2000, *Pastoral Care Emergencies*, St Louis, MS: Baker Academic; also Howard W. Stone, 1976, *Crisis Counselling*, Philadelphia: Fortress Press.

It is wise to recognize that this kind of ministry at times of acute strain, although potentially a source of rich fulfilment, will be also inevitably draining. The humble minister knows that her effectiveness for others depends more than anything else on the security of her own spiritual attachment to God. It is only as she goes on learning to plumb the depths of her own human vulnerability that she will develop sufficient spiritual poise and self-awareness to venture a holding and healing ministry to other troubled souls.

Healing and wholeness

Historically, the Church has always offered a rich and diverse range of ministries of healing and wholeness.[3] From the ancient traditions of care and hospitality undertaken by monastic communities, to more recent professional developments in fields such as hospital chaplaincy, Christians have ministered to the sick through prayer and sacrament, counsel and practical care, bringing the felt presence of covenantal love into the lives of suffering people through compassionate action and, above all, pastoral presence.

It is not immediately obvious, however, how best to relate a contemporary ministry of spiritual healing to the dominant biomedical paradigms of physical treatment and cure. Popular misunderstandings of Christian healing abound. At one extreme is the naive supernaturalism which embraces uncritical theologies of miraculous healing in an attempt to compete with secular treatments through a show of triumphalist and charismatic power. At the other extreme is the theologically vacuous pursuit of the kind of pseudo-professionalism which tries to 'baptize' secular techniques, for example in psychotherapeutic counselling, by giving them a veneer of spiritual respectability without any attempt to grapple theologically with their underlying anthropological presuppositions.

It is beyond the scope of this book to critique these distortions in rigorous detail. More constructively, we might consider how a theological understanding of life in all its fullness might provide a touchstone of integrity by which to evaluate our pastoral practice in this area. (See Chapter 2 for a full discussion of theological anthropology.) This perspective will help us in shaping a properly Christian approach to healing and wholeness amid the realities of life in all its

---

3 For a thorough historical review, see Amanda Porterfield, 2005, *Healing in the History of Christianity*, Oxford: Oxford University Press.

times and seasons, life in all its frustration and fragility, life in all its mutuality and communion and life in all its hope and potential.

On this account of human wholeness, we can begin to imagine how ministries of spiritual healing work to address the brokenness which is in some way out of step with life's times and seasons; unable to integrate life's frustration and fragility; alienated from life's mutuality and communion or incapable of embracing life's hope and potential. Whether it is through the simplest ministry of visiting the lonely or in the most sensitive ministries of pastoral counselling and reconciliation, the aim of any authentically Christian work of healing and wholeness will be to deepen and renew the kind of attachment to God through which the faith and hope and love of human beings made in God's image begins to be restored.

These principles are of the utmost importance when sharing a ministry of healing and wholeness with the dying and bereaved.

Walking the valley

The manifold skills and sensitivities of pastoral care – theological and ethical, personal and sacramental – are rarely so richly engaged as in the ministry of journeying alongside people towards their death. In the history of Christian pastoral care, the Church has regarded ministry to the dying as one of its highest priorities. Today, in our seemingly more secular age, the influence of the hospice and palliative care movement has brought renewed emphasis to the importance of spiritual ministry for those approaching death.

Cicely Saunders coined the memorable phrase 'total pain' to indicate the holistic challenge of easing suffering at the end of life, when physical pain may be only one aspect of a much broader anguish relating to multifaceted social, emotional and spiritual concerns. Although the latter dimensions may be less amenable to clear-cut description or diagnosis, there is a growing body of research which informs a pastoral understanding of spiritual 'pain'. Whether practising believers or not, human beings in the face of death have a need for hope, meaning and forgiveness – both in relation to the past and present and also in light of a dimly imagined future.

It is a remarkable privilege to be invited to walk alongside a person in the valley of the shadow of death – to learn from them, since none of us has walked that road ahead of others, and to offer whatever small gestures of care may bring sustenance for their journey. In this final pilgrimage of wholeness and healing, the role for a Christian minister may be considered under seven headings.

Companion

Dying is a uniquely lonely affair; and the path that leads away from all familiar and comforting relationships is hard for mortal human beings to tread. The minister's personal visit is therefore one of the most meaningful acts of pastoral presence. It is also the most profoundly human response of basic companionship. (The word *companionship* reminds us etymologically that as fellow mortals we share the same bread, and as fellow Christians we feast on the same bread of heaven.) Whether or not the pastor brings the sacramental gift of eucharistic ministry it is her simple presence – being there – with a willingness to share something of the instinctive dread of the abyss, which provides hope and encouragement that the dying person is not left to face the darkness alone.

Carer

The most basic elements of care – giving time, offering touch, with deep and generous attentiveness – take on a heightened significance when life itself is ebbing away. The personal presence of the pastor, face to face with the dying soul, speaks of the unfailing covenant of God's care. And because of the representative nature of her role, each small gesture of care can enrich and sustain the bonds of attachment to an eternal and undying love.

Comforter

From the original meaning of the word, this aspect of ministry is more about giving strength than offering consolation. Dying is hard work: and the dying soul needs spiritual resources that will sustain her on the journey. The simplest words and symbols can bring enormous comfort, but only if they are accessible to the person concerned. This is not the time for extended philosophical debate, but for basic crumbs of comfort which are meaningful and sustaining to the hungry spirit. The sensitive pastor will take her cue from careful listening and prayerful discernment. Surprisingly often the most elementary liturgical fragments – a remembrance of childhood hymns, the familiar phrases of the Lord's Prayer, the simple touch of prayerful anointing – will re-engage a primordial attachment to the deepest roots of faith.

Confessor

Making peace with the past is often the prerequisite to finding peace in the arms of God. For those schooled in the practice of a Catholic faith, the gift of formal absolution by a priest can bring immense healing as death approaches. For Christians of other traditions, as well as for many more who do not think of themselves as religious, the opportunity to unburden themselves in the presence of someone who represents the reconciling ministry of the Church can bring unexpected relief, with a sense of grateful acceptance that some of life's 'unfinished business' can finally be laid aside.

Counsellor

Facing up to the past can release fresh energies to grapple with the awesome challenges of the present. The pastor as counsellor offers her best skills of prayerful listening in the *kairos* time of final struggles, evaluations and decisions, when the last acts and intentions of a life that has run its course present a richly rewarding opportunity for gratitude, blessing and release.

Commender

At the bedside of a dying person, the Christian minister treads on holy ground. As the concerns of life's past and present give way to beckoning intimations of eternity, her prayerful presence holds open the door that stands between earth and heaven. Using time-honoured words of commendation, or rough-hewn prayers of the heart; alone, or in company with supporting family and friends; aloud, or in the silence of a watchful spirit; it is her privilege to commend to God's love and mercy the soul who sets forth on her final journey home.

Contemplative

> Who is sufficient for these things? (2 Cor. 2.16)

No matter how sophisticated her theology or how well-honed her counselling skills, every honest minister will tremble with inadequacy before the ultimate mysteries of death and eternity. In her ministry to the dying, the humble pastor can be almost unbearably exposed to doubt, hollowness and confusion. It is therefore only in stillness, prayer and naked trust in God that the contemplative minister will be replenished with deep wells of quiet courage for this awesome, but astonishingly beautiful ministry of love.

Picking up the pieces

> **A prayer for those who mourn**
>
> O God who brought us to birth,
> and in whose arms we die:
> in our grief and shock
> contain and comfort us;
> embrace us with your love,
> give us hope in our confusion,
> and grace to let go into new life,
> through Jesus Christ. Amen.
>
> Janet Morley[4]

---

4 Janet Morley, 1992, *All Desires Known*, London: SPCK, p. 87.

Approaches to healing and wholeness in pastoral care of the bereaved have been informed by a vast amount of research into the complex and overwhelming processes of human grief. Tidy-minded theorists sometimes imagine that the confusing experiences of grief can be systematized into a simple framework of memorable psychological phases. By analogy with the predictable stages by which physical wounds heal, for example, Colin Murray Parkes in 1972 used attachment theory to construct an orderly sequence of responses through which the emotional wounds of grief could be envisaged to 'heal' over the course of months and years.

His widely known model, along with the descriptions of other bereavement experts, sheds some helpful light on the dark inner landscape of grief – the initial numbness and denial; the yearning and raw loneliness that is often physically as well as spiritually painful; the disorganization and despair of a life that has lost its bearings; and the eventual quiet movement towards acceptance, readaptation and new purpose in living. Finding a language to describe the sometimes alarming symptoms of acute and persistent grief can be a useful tool to foster empathy with those who mourn, helping them to know that they are not alone in their distress.[5]

Yet, sensitive pastors recognize that no tidy structure is likely to do justice to the inherently chaotic experience of grief, in which the whole orientation of both inner and outer worlds may be painfully disrupted. The best that theoretical models of bereavement can offer is to augment the limited experience and understanding of carers; but it is a mistake to imagine that scientific tools alone will provide a shortcut to deep listening, searching faith and costly, personal care. In the final part of this chapter, we shall turn therefore to the wider pastoral question of how the whole Christian community is called to share in the profoundly hope-full task of 'picking up the pieces' of loss.

---

5 For a recent summary of theories of bereavement see Elisabeth Kübler-Ross and David Kessler, 2005, *On Grief and Grieving: Finding the Meaning of Grief Through the Five Stages of Loss*, London: Simon & Schuster.

> **Pastoral Story**
>
> Beverley was a middle-aged African-Caribbean woman whose husband, Joe, died suddenly of a heart attack. Although she had no previous links with her local church, she appreciated the kindness shown to her at her husband's funeral and started to attend the Sunday morning services from time to time.
>
> About six months after the funeral, Beverley broke down in tears at the end of a service. She told Sheila, one of the welcoming team, that it would have been Joe's birthday that week. She felt terribly lonely and was struggling to go on with life without him.
>
> Sheila was able to invite Beverley to her home for lunch on the day of Joe's birthday. They talked together about all kinds of memories, and Beverley said that she wanted to light a birthday candle for Joe in the church. Later in the day they went together to the church. Beverley lit a candle, and the pastoral worker offered a simple prayer of healing, thankfulness and peace.
>
> Through tears and laughter, lighting up his birthday candle against the darkness of grief, Sheila joined with Beverley in a profoundly pastoral act of solidarity to sing 'Happy Birthday' one last time for her Joe.

Christians believe in a love that conquers death. This faith is not an abstract doctrine about an unimaginable future destiny, but a solid conviction about the healing power of undying love which binds all God's people together in hope. This deep conviction expresses itself just as much in practical gestures of compassion as in sensitive theological reflection. It is not the sole preserve of ordained ministers, but is a natural part of the witness of the whole Church.

- Informal befriending and social networks;
- Bereavement groups and courses;
- Pastoral visiting schemes;
- Regular prayers to remember the dead;
- Bereavement services, especially at All Souls' in November.

All these humble gestures of pastoral care testify to the solidarity in suffering and hope that is the Christian's enduring legacy. 'The end is gain, of course,' wrote Marjorie Allingham in the light of her own grief. 'Blessed are they that mourn, for they shall be made strong, in fact. But the process is like all human births, painful and long and dangerous.'[6]

Being human, being there, being good news

There are many specialist ministries of pastoral care and counselling which some priests and ministers are trained to offer for work with the sick and suffering, the dying and bereaved. It is not the purpose of this book to survey in any detail the knowledge and competencies which are required of those who provide a professional level of care, in the context of appropriate referral, for people with complex physical or mental health concerns, people struggling with complicated grief, or people seeking the grace of sacramental confession. No pastor should expect to work beyond her limits.

This chapter has sought to orientate the humble pastor with sufficient compassionate wisdom for a demanding, yet remarkably fulfilling, area of pastoral care. In the face of sadness, crisis and grief, the core elements of Christian pastoral care remain terribly simple: being human, being there and being good news.

Questions

'Even though I walk through the darkest valley, I fear no evil; for you are with me; your rod and your staff – they comfort me.' (Ps. 23.4)

- What do you think a 'good death' would be?
- What does Christian hope mean to you?
- What do you think are the essential qualities for someone who visits the bereaved on behalf of the Church?

---

6 From Marjorie Allingham, 1952, *Tiger in the Smoke*, London: Chatto & Windus, quoted in Agnes Whitaker (ed.), 1989, *All in the End is Harvest*, London: Darton, Longman and Todd, p. 123.

Further Reading

Ainsworth-Smith, Ian and Peter Speck, 1982, *Letting Go: Caring for the Dying and Bereaved*, London: SPCK.
Billings, Alan, 2002, *Dying and Grieving: A Guide to Pastoral Ministry*, London: SPCK.
Bowlby, Richard, 2004, *Fifty Years of Attachment Theory*, London: Karnac Books.
Brueggemann, Walter, 1984, *The Message of the Psalms*, Minneapolis: Augsburg Fortress Press.
Cassidy, Sheila, 1988, *Sharing the Darkness: The Spirituality of Caring*, London: Darton, Longman and Todd.
Cobb, Mark, 2001, *The Dying Soul: Spiritual Care at the End of Life*, Buckingham: Open University Press.
Evans, Abigail R., 2011, *Is God Still at the Bedside? The Medical, Ethical, and Pastoral Issues of Death and Dying*, Grand Rapids: Eerdmans.
Kelly, Ewan, 2008, *Meaningful Funerals: Meeting the Theological and Pastoral Challenge in a Postmodern Era*, London: Mowbray.
Kübler-Ross, Elisabeth and David Kessler, 2005, *On Grief and Grieving: Finding the Meaning of Grief Through the Five Stages of Loss*, London: Simon & Schuster.
Lewis, C. S., 1961, *A Grief Observed*, New York: Harper & Row.
Nouwen, Henri J. M., 1982, *A Letter of Consolation*, San Francisco: HarperCollins.
Parkes, Colin Murray, 2006, *The Roots of Grief and its Complications*, London: Routledge.
Stump, Eleonore, 2012, *Wandering in Darkness: Narrative and the Problem of Suffering*, Oxford: Oxford University Press.
Swinton, John, 2007, *Raging with Compassion: Pastoral Responses to the Problem of Evil*, Grand Rapids: Eerdmans.
Switzer, David, 2000, *Pastoral Care Emergencies*, St Louis, MS: Baker Academic.
Whitaker, Agnes (ed.), 1989, *All in the End is Harvest*, London: Darton, Longman and Todd.
Wolterstorff, Nicholas, 1987, *Lament for a Son*, Grand Rapids: Eerdmans.
Woodward, James, 2005, *Befriending Death*, London: SPCK.

6

Growing Together
Religion, Relationships and Ritual

The pastoral ministry of the Church is sometimes mistakenly seen as dealing primarily with individuals in need. This is quite a dangerous misconception which owes more to our modern Western culture of individualism than to a fully theological understanding of human flourishing.[1] With this temptation in mind, one of the overriding concerns of this book is to emphasize the inherently relational calling of the gospel and the irreducibly corporate nature of growth to Christian maturity. Pastoral care is always about growing together.

This chapter concludes the first part of the book which sets out a theological agenda for life in all its fullness. We shall explore God's call to human beings to live and grow together in community. We shall then consider some of the pastoral aspects of group dynamics within the life of the church community and explore the immense significance of shared ritual and worship in the overall ecology of Christian pastoral care.

---

1 For a trenchant critique of the excessive individualism of some expressions of pastoral care and counselling, see Stephen Pattison, 2000, *A Critique of Pastoral Care*, London: SCM.

Sinews and ligaments

Some of the most unglamorous elements in the living body are surely those hidden strings which tie together the bones and joints of the human skeleton. The humble sinews and ligaments of the body are anatomically no more than bits of grey gristle, but such is their toughness and flexibility that they provide for an astonishing degree of articulated power and resilience.

In his well-known analogy of the Body of Christ, Paul pays especial attention to the indispensable part played by these connecting sinews and ligaments, which hold everything together in order that the whole body may grow (Col. 2.19; Eph. 4.16). In an individualistic age, it can be easy for Christians to overlook the importance of the bonds of attachment and connection which are vital to our shared life and maturity in the Body of Christ.

Christian faith can never be a private pursuit. Our calling to be human in Christ is an invitation to a life of communion and mutuality with others; and it is in and through our encounters with others, by the grace of the Holy Spirit, that we are drawn towards maturity in the love of God. For pastors, therefore, a concern for the health and vitality of the church body is inseparable from a commitment to the care and nurture of individual members. Every minister needs to be alert to the social, ecclesial and political contexts which shape and embody the bonds of attachment to Christ through which the whole Church is organically nurtured towards fullness of life.

The most basic organic priority is for the Church to be an open and inclusive community. The Body of Christ welcomes people of all backgrounds and races into the Church. But we are called to much more than this as a community of persons in the image of God-in-Trinity. We also need to think creatively about how the distinctive vocation of each person can be fostered as a source of mutual enrichment and delight. This is the connective role of sinews and ligaments through which different hopes and histories come to be held and knit together. Through mutual relationships of pastoral encouragement and concern, the whole Church can then fulfil her potential as a living, growing sacrament of trinitarian love.

Pastoral Story

St Augustine's was a small town centre church in an area of urban decline. Few families remained in the neighbourhood; and the remnant which made up the dwindling congregation came mostly from surrounding suburbs. After years of struggling to sustain an active mission with few local leadership resources, the church authorities finally decided that St Augustine's would have to close.

A small group of worshippers from St Augustine's made a tentative approach to a nearby church in the parish of All Saints. The vicar there was deeply sympathetic to their situation, understanding the sadness and exhaustion that they were experiencing after years of trying to revive a slowly dying church community. She attended the final service of thanksgiving at St Augustine's and was humbled to learn how much dedication had been poured into the church's life over decades.

In the coming months a few former members started to worship at All Saints. Initially it was hard for them to feel at home, though they were glad to have laid down an impossible burden of responsibility. Several people made particular efforts to befriend and welcome them, without pressure, to get involved in the life of their new church. Barry, their former churchwarden, was invited onto the PCC; and Mary, their former organist, brought along her young grandson to join the choir. On Sundays the life and ministry of St Augustine's was regularly recalled in the prayers; and from time to time one of the favourite hymns from the old church was included in the service.

Sadly, some members of All Saints felt that rather too much attention was being lavished on the newcomers. They said that All Saints should be looking forwards, not back. Most people however appreciated the honoured place that was accorded to a group of fellow-Christians with a unique story of God's unfailing guidance. They were grateful to sense that, through the gift of their presence at All Saints, the whole church was becoming a more generous and inclusive community.

The ties that bind

The word for 'religion' comes from a Latin root which means 'to bind fast'. The insights of social psychology help us to appreciate how much more there is to living a religious life than simply holding on to a set of cognitive beliefs. Being a member of a faith community entails a significant set of human connections and attachments which bind people together in shared moral and emotional commitments of loyalty, respect and reverence. What is more, for Christians who are baptized into the life of the 'one, holy, catholic, and apostolic Church' of the creed, their ties of faith will cut across some of the deepest divisions in society, binding together believers from every age and class and culture in one great family of God.

This organic interconnectedness may be expressed institutionally through membership of a specific local church community. We cannot underestimate the importance of this corporate dimension. In a highly mobile society, where membership of voluntary groups is rarely durable, the willingness of Christian people to stay faithful to the life and service of a local church can be a distinctive witness and a real source of social as well as spiritual 'capital' in any neighbourhood. The local church may not be the only context for collective Christian practice, however, and many people look to wider networks for different kinds of spiritual encouragement, friendship and pastoral care. The appeal of such new social forms and communities, including 'virtual' communities of faith, has been harnessed by the ecumenical movement for 'Fresh Expressions' of Church.

In an age that is marked by privatization of faith, it is not surprising to find patterns of Christian belonging that are pluriform and sometimes highly ambiguous. Whether or not the members of our society profess a strong personal faith, and whether or not people themselves attend worship on a regular basis, it is not at all uncommon to find a residual sense of emotional attachment to the Church and all that it stands for – even if this sense of connection is expressed with ambivalence or even hostility. Amid such complex attitudes and reactions to the idea of 'Church', it is vital for pastors to recognize the subtle dynamics which play out in relation to a group or community which holds immense symbolic and public representative meaning.

Respecting group identity

How can we begin to make sense of these complex and contradictory emotional and spiritual attachments which the Church seems to elicit? One of the basic insights of social psychology is that group entities function as a major source of social identity. Our human sense of who we are, and what we stand for, is strongly coloured by identification with social groups of various kinds. The depth of our identification with different groups varies, however, and there will be some communities in which we feel a much deeper sense of personal investment than others.

A simple distinction can be drawn between primary and secondary groups in terms of the nature of their bonding power. A *primary group*, such as the family, is based on intimate relationships which endure over many years; whereas *secondary groups*, such as working communities, are typically more formal and institutional in nature and may disband once their task is achieved. Sociologists find that the primary group is of far deeper significance in terms of identity and is the community to which human beings look primarily for care and emotional support and a sense of enduring personal concern.[2]

Which kind of group is the Church? For many people their pattern of relating to the Church might suggest a rather loose kind of attachment, more typical of a secondary group than a primary group. They may come and go in terms of church attendance, perhaps sitting quite lightly in terms of functional engagement with church life. And yet there is often a deeper underlying sense of the idea of 'Church' and all that it dimly represents in terms of a sacred and caring presence which resonates with primitive feelings of attachment that have much more in common with the relationships of a primary group.

Theologically we might speak of these contradictory social dynamics in terms of *vicarious* believing. The idea that ministers and active worshippers offer regular prayers and sustain the presence of sacred spaces on behalf of a wider community is quite deeply embedded in the history of British pastoral care. It may be derided, of course, from time to time, but even the light-hearted request to 'say one for me' reveals a residual, rather poignant, sense of tenuous attachment to a faithfully worshipping community.

---

2 See Charles Cooley, 1909, *Social Organization: A Study of the Larger Mind*, New York: Charles Scribner's Sons.

In a fascinating discussion of 'vicarious faith or religion-lite', John Saxbee recalls that vicariousness goes to the heart of what Jesus was about in his life and in his death.[3] Jesus' solidarity with the whole of humanity, which is never imposed or intrusive, is the source of a generous grace which spills out in healing and forgiveness to many who feel far removed from the presence of God's love. Rather than grumbling, then, about the looseness of the bonds which nominal Christians demonstrate towards the Church, Saxbee encourages a hospitable vision of pastoral care which is glad to minister in good grace to those who retain some vestigial sense of connection to the community of God's people.

Serving the Body of Christ through pastoral care, then, has a far wider reach than is often supposed. The relational genius of the Christian faith creates what Robert Putnam describes as a kind of 'bridging' social capital as well as the more inward-looking 'bonding' social capital among its regular membership.[4] A sense of the depth and breadth of attachment which the Church represents is therefore crucial if pastors are not to underestimate the enormous potential for good or harm in the presence and practice of their ministry within the wider community.

The closure of a church offers a telling example of these attachments. When a parish church like St Augustine's is closed down, the body blow is felt not only by the remnant of regular worshippers, but also within a wider community which grieves the loss of a Christian presence in their neighbourhood. The kindness and sensitivity with which the people of All Saints tried to heal this wound reflects a deep respect and keen awareness of the pastoral importance of the church community in their area.

Understanding group behaviour

The ebbs and flows of communal life are not always plain sailing, of course, and the ways in which human communities not only reflect individual human reactions, but also amplify their emotional resonance, can give rise to complicated dynamics within the lives of churches and congregations.

---

3 John Saxbee, 2009, *No Faith in Religion*, Ropley: O Books, pp. 85–95.

4 Robert D. Putnam, 2000, *Bowling Alone: The Collapse and Retrieval of American Community*, New York: Simon and Schuster.

One of the perceptive insights of group theory is that the feelings and communications expressed within the dynamics of the group operate at a deep and powerful emotional level. At this level of attachment behaviour, which is often unconscious, the group behaves as much more than a collection of individuals, acting out systemic moods and primitive feelings which come to dominate the life of an entire social group. As we shall see below, these group dynamics are felt with particular force in the context of ritual and worship, where they have a heightened capacity either to heal or to harm.

At a more everyday level, group theorists have described the dynamic cycles which are typical for any community which provides some sort of 'comfort zone' for its members. The well-known theory of Bruce Tuckman explains some of the common shifts in corporate mood in terms of the stages in a group life cycle that proceed from 'forming', 'storming', 'norming' and 'performing' to final 'adjourning' or 'mourning' as the unit of social significance finally breaks up.[5]

Transition and change is an unsettling experience for groups and institutions, just as much as for individuals, who must face the disruption and challenges of new growth. Sensitive pastors learn how to read and respect the significant shifts that take place in the emotional and spiritual landscape of churches and neighbourhoods, seeking to encourage healing and growth through times of major readjustment.

The power of ritual to hold and transform a community at such sensitive times can be immensely important. Amid the loss and disappointment that accompanies the closing down of a once-lively Christian community, for example, a service of thanksgiving can acknowledge and entrust to God all that has been precious to many generations of worshippers. It allows space for mourning and builds new solidarities, which strengthen people to withstand the dislocation and adjustment of seeking a new spiritual home.

For the faithful remnant of St Augustine's, there was an ongoing need for pastoral care and encouragement as each individual had to negotiate the uncertainties and conflicts of relating to a new community. Their integration into the life of All Saints involved some inevitable awkwardnesses of 'forming, storming and norming'. The quiet reassurance that came from gentle and patient pastoral support was hugely appreciated throughout this time of transition, building

---

5 Bruce Tuckman, 1965, 'Developmental Sequence in Small Groups', *Psychological Bulletin* 63 (6), pp. 384–99.

hope and confidence that their faith would not only survive, but flourish, in the new situation to which God was calling them.

Healing group anxiety

To be a person in relationship is to be caught up into the current of other people's emotional and spiritual dynamics. In the previous chapter we have seen through our consideration of attachment theory that strong primary relationships offer the foundation for deep levels of human security which reflect, in some measure, the faithful covenant love of the eternal Trinity. For this reason, the communal life of the church can resonate, sometimes overwhelmingly, with the profound forces of attachment behaviour which play out in feelings of deep security, or alternatively, of disturbing anxiety.

In certain respects, therefore, it can be instructive to compare the dynamics of church life with those of a family system. Research in social psychology has identified many of the hidden and complex forces which operate in the systemic life of human families, often with shocking intensity. It is important to take a systemic perspective when trying to reckon with processes which seem to magnify feelings, especially where it seems that the reactions of a group come to transcend the sum of the responses of the individual represented within it.

A common example of this systemic behaviour relates to the manifestations of group anxiety. Christian people may feel at some very primitive level that the church, rather like the family, is a safe womb within which the most fundamental personal and spiritual anxieties will be safely held. But what happens, then, when the church itself goes through choppy waters? How can this spiritual anxiety be handled?

In a very telling story from the Gospels, we see a group of disciples caught up in a furious storm on Lake Galilee. They turn desperately to Jesus to save them from their fears. A sense of overwhelming panic seems to grip the whole company. And it is only the serenity and spiritual authority of Jesus which is able to restore calm and a renewed sense of security (Matt. 8.23–27). While not imagining themselves as in any sense miracle-workers, many pastors similarly discover that a vital part of their role is to provide the reassurance that contains the anxiety not only of troubled individuals, but even more so of families and communities in turmoil.

This role has parallels with the way that psychodynamic counsellors speak of bringing a 'non-anxious presence' in order to foster healing and growth in disturbed family systems. Particularly where the anxieties of a whole family come to be projected, perhaps disproportionately, onto one member, then the role of the professional in defusing systemic anxiety can be a great resource for restoring a sense of trust and equilibrium. Something very similar can be seen in the ups and downs of life in the church.

Once more we recall the important function of those unobtrusive 'sinews and ligaments' which bear the strains of connectivity in order to hold the whole body together in love. From a theological perspective, Paul's image reminds us that the health and growth of the entire body is guaranteed because of its living connection to the head (Col. 2.19; Eph. 4.15–16). Within the systemic life of the church, it is the covenantal attachment of each member to the unbreakable bonds of Christ's love which promises ultimate confidence and maturity. The special role of pastors, often in deeply unseen and unglamorous ministries, is to keep people lovingly connected to Christ and to one another.

In the overall ecology of pastoral care it is the human connectivity of the church, fleshed out in organic relationships through homes and families, neighbourhoods and workplaces, as well as through wider socio-political witness for a just and peaceful society, which makes the gospel call to fullness of life in Christ not only intelligible, but powerfully attractive. This invitation to a corporate participation in the grace of God is extended most richly through the experiences of Christian worship. With this in view, we turn in the next part of this chapter to reflect on the role of ritual in pastoral care.

Ritual and pastoral care

The opening ceremony for the London Olympics in 2012 culminated in a memorable piece of ritual action. Tens of thousands watched live and millions more on television, as the flame that had been carried all around Great Britain was brought into the waiting stadium where it would light up the cauldron to mark the official launch of the thirtieth Olympiad. In an act of glorious symbolism, the torchbearer's flame was passed to seven teenagers who each lit a single tiny flame within a copper petal on the ground. As the world watched with bated breath fresh flames caught fire in over 200 copper petals which rose up into the air as one flame, creating a glorious fiery cauldron of global unity. In an age which is felt to be ignorant or impatient of ritual this magnificent spectacle generated a powerful experience of human solidarity and hope.

Human ritual goes back a long way. Ceremonial actions can be traced back to the earliest expressions of human cultural life and religious worship. Over 3,000 years ago, the ancient Greek mystery religions crafted sacred rites made up of symbolic actions and processions (*drōmena*), the presentation of hallowed objects (*deiknumena*), and the incantation of words of interpretation (*legomena*), to express a depth of communal meaning which transcended the functional interactions of everyday social life.

Ritual plays a vital role in pastoral care. In the ecology of Christian living it should not surprise us that shared ritual makes a significant contribution to the feeding and nurturing, healing and guiding of the whole community towards maturity of life in Christ. Ritual enactments may be formal or informal, linguistically elaborate or richly non-verbal, heady with music or quivering with silence, steeped in ancient symbolism or pregnant with evocative new meanings. Whether small scale and intimate, or vast and theatrical, the power of ritual works to release deep unconscious forces from the individual and collective soul.

Elaine Ramshaw draws from research in psychology and anthropology to identify five aspects of the role of ritual in the life of a community.[6] First, there is a role in the *establishing of order* which works to undergird the experience of life together with a sense of stability and purpose, security and hope. In this respect, there is something profoundly reassuring about the stylized, time-honoured and repetitive nature of ritual, which communicates a sense of enduring value at an emotional level far deeper than words.

Second, the power of ritual serves to *reaffirm meaning* by the repetition of symbolic actions week by week and year by year and by lending especial gravitas and significance at times of crisis and major transition. It is important that ritual should be serious, without gimmicks or fakery. The quality and integrity of ritual works at deeply subconscious levels, bringing together and affirming disparate visions of goodness and truth, in a rich integration of powerfully attractive shared symbols.

Third, and crucially for pastoral care, ritual works to *bond the community*. This is especially evident in the Christian sacraments. Creating a hospitable

---

6 See Elaine Ramshaw, 1986, *Ritual and Pastoral Care*, Philadelphia: Fortress Press, pp. 23–34.

space, sacramental rituals work to shape a kind of shared spiritual home, providing a wonderful example of how ritual can draw people together in unity and love. Evoking deeply subconscious attachment behaviours, a ritual such as the Holy Communion speaks to the individual and collective imagination about the heavenly home where all are welcome and everyone shall be fed.

Psychologists point out that there is also a darkness about ritual representation which enables the more subtle function of *handling ambivalence* in the psyche of individuals and the community. This aspect of ritual reflects psychoanalytic understandings of how deep-seated conflicts and shadow sides of human experience can be integrated at a level which goes deeper than everyday rationalistic language. Holding together both neediness and strength, sinfulness and forgiveness, the spiritual dynamic of effective ritual dispenses a mighty power through some of the simplest actions of public worship, such as the absolution of sins or the pronouncing of a formal blessing.

The final core function of ritual is to bring us to the edge of the abyss, to the *encounter with mystery*. This numinous dimension of worship connects with the earliest infantile experiences of bliss and wonder in the gaze of a loving parent or the profound reassurance felt in the exchange of a gracious touch. It would be easy to underestimate the phenomenal power of corporate worship to transform the deepest levels of human consciousness, both individually and collectively. Preachers or worship leaders who are too prosaic or pedestrian can be blind to the intimate forces of redemptive grace which work at a primal level, far below the surface rational layers of thought and language. These are the hidden dynamics of worship: sacred music and rich colour, ancient symbol and rhythmic movement. Within the deep pastoral ecology of effective worship, this is the place of encounter with the mysterious Holy Spirit in the unconscious, sub-rational and emotive parts of the soul where the deepest healing of human imagination waits to be discovered.

Human rites

A sensitivity to the dynamics of ritual is especially important for pastors, who are called to accompany people through the great times and seasons and transition points of human life. Whether as priests and worship leaders, or through ministries of preparation and support for special occasions such as baptism, first communion, marriage or funeral, pastors are privileged to come alongside people, when major human turning points are marked out in ritual ways within the worshipping life of the church.

Anthropologists describe these significant ritual occasions as *rites of passage*. Research from a wide variety of human cultures reveals a pattern of ritualization which helps to support and make sense of major shifts in the relationship of individuals and communities. Typically at crucial times of the life cycle, such as birth, puberty, marriage or death, it seems that different cultures and religions develop a pattern of ritual behaviour which lends a depth of communal meaning to far-reaching changes in family and social life.

Figure 6.1 Rites of passage

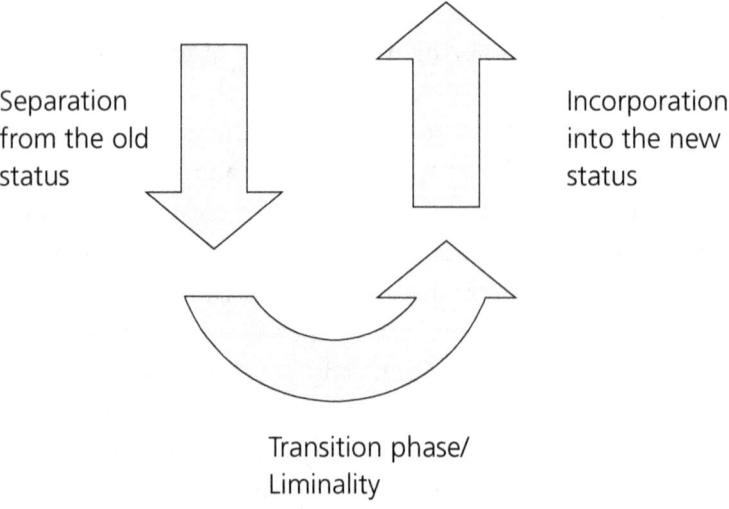

Separation from the old status

Incorporation into the new status

Transition phase/ Liminality

Arnold van Gennep defined the pattern of these rites of passage in terms of three phases which demarcate a separation from the old status, a phase of transition and an incorporation into the new status. Victor Turner expanded on this initial work, paying deeper attention to the way in which the fuzzy liminal stage, the phase of transition, was handled.[7] In a religious context, as we saw in Chapter 3, it is this phase of transition – or liminality – which can be of especial spiritual

---

7 Arnold van Gennep, 1960, *The Rites of Passage*, translated by M. B. V. and G. L. Caffee, Chicago: University of Chicago Press; Victor Turner, 1969, *The Ritual Process: Structure and Anti-Structure*, New York: Aldine de Gruyter.

significance. According to Gordon Lynch the liminal stage entails a degree of disengagement, disidentification, disenchantment and disorientation.[8] Human beings who are passing through this 'molten' phase of liminality, when past identities and understandings are breaking down and new possibilities and relationships are coming to birth, turn instinctively to prayer and worship for the resources that will help them on the path towards greater maturity.

The churches have an important ministry of hospitality in opening up the resources of a living faith to individuals and families who are negotiating the major transitions of life. Of course, it is not always easy to reconcile the purely social or familial function of rites of passage with the spiritual significance of the traditional Christian sacraments. This kind of tension may be played out, for example, in the differing understandings which people bring to an event described either as a 'christening' or a 'baptism'. Although these tensions can be hard to resolve doctrinally, it is interesting to reflect on the way in which the ritual itself can accommodate a wide range of symbolic meanings. Unlike the precise terms of language which define and separate different understandings of reality, ritual 'tries to reassert the connectedness of things, and the continuities of life, [being] less an expression of thought than an experiment in living'.[9]

Such insights are enormously helpful in the pastoral context of identifying and responding to ritual needs. In a predominantly post-Christian culture, pastors need sensitivity and imagination to connect with people who still look towards the Church to provide some kind of transcendent framework of meaning for occasions of celebration or of sadness. This kind of ministry is not restricted to the traditional 'occasional offices' of the parish church.

- A children's ministry team creates an awesome worship experience through Godly Play.
- A local vicar crafts a joyful house blessing for newcomers to the neighbourhood.
- A hospital chaplain works with bereaved parents to co-construct a sensitive and personal liturgy after the birth of their stillborn baby.
- A school chaplain devises special services to mark the beginning and end of the school year.

---

8 Gordon Lynch, 2002, *Pastoral Care and Counselling*, London: Sage, p. 191.
9 Cheslyn Jones, Geoffrey Wainwright and Edward Yarnold (eds), 1978, *The Study of Liturgy*, London: SPCK, p. 57.

- A long-serving priest welcomes married couples back to church to a special Mass to celebrate their golden wedding anniversary.

In all these situations and many more, pastors use their ritual skills to weave connections between half-belief and shared faith in ways which deeply affirm the importance of human experience and demonstrate the present reality of God's faithful care. An understanding of psychological and cultural forces gives depth to our pastoral instincts about how best to accompany people through these major turning points of life.

These forces should always be handled with care. We need to be alert to the power that is exerted by worship leaders and others who lead people through the intense processes of ritual experience: and we shall return to these issues more critically in Chapter 9. At this point we acknowledge with care and respect the enormous reworking of the soul that takes place in the liminal moments of profound worship. When the inner life of a human being is melted down, like a chrysalis, through the gracious stirrings of the Holy Spirit, then the work of the pastor must be humble and reverent and never intrusive. We tread on holy ground.

Caring together

Pastoral theology is the study of how and why Christians care; and this care has irreducibly corporate, social and ritual dimensions. In this chapter, we have reflected on the practical wisdom underlying some of the complex relational dynamics within which human beings grow together towards maturity in their love for God and for one another. In the community of the church, and especially in her life of worship, these subtle dynamics gather a depth of spiritual and psychic energy, which, if it is healthy and authentic, can be a powerful means of transforming grace.

A large view of pastoral care needs to engage with these human realities in a spirit of ecclesial intelligence, relational openheartedness and profound sensitivity to ritual. Above all, the pastor seeks to share her own humanity with others in the mutual communion that is the touchstone of life together in Christ. It is not a matter of bringing a detached interpretation or superior analysis to bear on the human lives and interactions of others. The pastor prays for the wisdom to learn that all of us human beings are in this together and for the grace to work out her own vocation in open-hearted love and genuine humility.

In the first half of this book, we have laid the foundations of pastoral care in a theological understanding of human nature and the call to grow to maturity in Christ. It is the great privilege of pastors to accompany people through many changes and challenges of life, working to affirm and to guide, to heal and to reconcile amid the passions, problems and potentials of human life in all its fullness, always seeking to build up the whole community of God's people in the life of the Spirit. In the second half of the book, we shall turn our thoughts more specifically to the practice of pastoral care as it has unfolded in the past and as it is being critically reappraised and developed in the contemporary Church.

Questions

- Where have you recognized some of the hidden forces that build up Christian community? What does this suggest to you about the nature of pastoral care?
- When have you experienced an act of worship as a time of 'molten' change and transformation? Is this always a sign of God's grace?
- What do you think are the most meaningful rites of passage in our contemporary society? How effectively does the church come alongside people with pastoral care at these times?

Further Reading

Anderson, Herbert and Edward Foley, 1998, *Mighty Stories, Dangerous Rituals: Weaving Together the Human and the Divine*, San Francisco: Jossey-Bass.

Bell, Catherine, 1997, *Ritual: Perspectives and Dimensions*, Oxford: Oxford University Press.

Brown, Rupert, 2000, *Group Processes*, 2nd ed., Oxford: Blackwell.

Deadman, Richard, Jeremy Fletcher, Janet Hudson and Stephen Oliver (eds), 1996, *Pastoral Prayers: A Resource for Pastoral Occasions*, London: Mowbray.

Grenz, Stanley, 1994, *Theology for the Community of God*, Carlisle: Paternoster.

Oliver, Gillian, 2012, *The Church Weddings Handbook: The Seven Pastoral Moments that Matter*, London: Church House Publishing.

Pembroke, Neil, 2010, *Pastoral Care in Worship*. London: T & T Clark.

Ramshaw, Elaine, 1986, *Ritual and Pastoral Care*, Philadelphia: Fortress Press.

Savage, Sara and Eolene Boyd-Macmillan, 2007, *The Human Face of the Church: A Social Psychology and Pastoral Theology Resource for Pioneer and Traditional Ministry*, Norwich: Canterbury Press.

Watts, Fraser, Rebecca Nye and Sara Savage, 2002, *Psychology for Christian Ministry*, London: Routledge.

Ward, Pete (ed.), 2004, *The Rite Stuff: Ritual in Contemporary Christian Worship and Mission*, Oxford: Bible Reading Fellowship.

Wells, Samuel and Sarah Coakley (eds), 2008, *Praying for England: Priestly Presence in Contemporary Culture*, London: Continuum.

Part 2

For Their Sakes: The Call to Care

7

Tend my Flock
The Story of Pastoral Care

The second part of this study guide turns from broad reflection about our common human calling in Christ to a more practical focus on the pastoral call to care.

At the beginning of the book, we recalled the story of God's covenant of care for his people. The steadfast stream of faithful loving-kindness, pouring forth from the heart of the Trinity, calls human beings into a responsive relationship of love for God and care for one another. This is the glorious theological reality which underlies the Christian calling to care – both within and beyond the life of the church community.

Over the centuries, Christians have worked out this magnificent vocation in a myriad of different ways. In its countless manifestations, we recognize that the offering of pastoral care is always provisional and contextual, being hammered out in practical situations of human struggle and joy, while boldly pointing forward to the fullness of life and redemption in the coming Kingdom of God. For now, we can gladly accept that the scope of Christian commitment is always appropriately limited, just as the vision of pastoral care is necessarily particular to a time and a place.

In this chapter, we shall trace some key moments in the history of pastoral care, which have been especially influential in relation to contemporary models of practice. And since this book has been written in a British context, we shall focus particularly on the distinctive characteristics of pastoral care which have taken root in this soil and have come to shape a typically British approach to pastoral theology.

A kind of loving

It is relatively easy, of course, to think about caring in a non-specific sort of way. We reviewed in Chapter 1 some of the generic features of caring which begin to shape the agenda for pastoral care in a broad-brush kind of way. But Christian love requires a commitment which is always concrete and particular. It is necessarily anchored in living relationships. It will not rest content with abstractions that are not earthed in real life. Theologically we can say that pastoral care is an embodied witness to the loving presence of God in the midst of ordinary human life. It will always need to be worked out on the ground; and in doing so it will need to enact the highly particular characteristics of *intercession, incarnation, intention, information* and *integration*.

'What kind of love is this?' asks John Pritchard in a recent book about priesthood.[1] His answer, which is equally valid for all Christian pastors and not only those who are ordained, points us first to 'a love that prays'. Today more than ever, Christians need to reclaim the *intercessory* basis of pastoral care. Very simply, it is the act of entrusting one another to God which is at the heart of our common life or *koinonia*. So, prayer is not an additional activity which is overlaid as a kind of afterthought on the real work of practical caring which takes place with no reference to the grace of God. Prayer is central to the pastor's identity and vital to the enactment of his role as someone who invites others, through humble ventures of care, to know the loving presence of God. Prayer cannot be seen as an adjunct. Whatever else the pastor does, or tries to do, with and for others, it will be his work of intercession which authenticates his or her ministry as part of the Church's unfolding witness to the transforming grace of God.

> ## Practice Point
>
> You can pray with them sometimes, but pray for them always.[2]

---

1 John Pritchard, 2007, *The Life and Work of a Priest*, London: SPCK, p. 7.
2 Attributed to Geoffrey Studdert-Kennedy, quoted in David Scott, 1997, *Moments of Prayer*, London: SPCK, p. 30.

A second hallmark of pastoral care points to its distinctively *incarnational* character. What does this mean in practice? We mentioned in Chapter 1 the significance of *being human* and *being there*: two fundamental characteristics by which Christian pastors bear witness to the presence of God who is always humbly at work in the world. The doctrine of the incarnation expresses the astonishing theological insight of God's humility. In his ongoing creation and re-creation of the world, the God of the covenant is not so much God-over-us but God-with-us, *Emmanuel*. This humble, incarnational vision shapes one of the distinctive features of pastoral ministry, as opposed to other more formal models of professional care, which is its essential messiness. Because pastoral care seeks to be embedded in the comings and goings of everyday life, it is its informality which is its greatest strength (and also, as we shall see, a necessary vulnerability).

We shall consider the challenges of the fuzzy edges of pastoral care more carefully in Chapter 9. At this point it is important to celebrate the value of the kind of low-key presence which is loving enough *not* to be overly demarcated or detached from the run of everyday life, but is glad to identify with the ordinariness of human relationships, especially in their weakness and poverty and suffering (Phil. 2.1–8).

Practice Point

Pastoral effectiveness consists more in sharing lives than in solving problems.

The challenge of this model of messy ministry is not to lose sight of its *intentionality*. We are sadly familiar with the caricature of the ineffectual parson of yesteryear, who whiled away his afternoons taking tea with parishioners, because he had nothing better to do! Such lack of focus is a travesty of genuine pastoral care which, in the words of David Scott's poem, is 'going about something quite different'. In its intentionality, therefore, pastoral care aims not merely to 'go about' in a purposeless way, but to 'go about doing good' (cf. Acts 10.38).

> **Parish Visit**
>
> Going about something quite different,
> begging quiet entrance
> with nothing in my bag, I land
> on the other side of the red painted step
> hoping things will take effect.
> The space in the house is ten months old
> and time has not yet filled it up,
> nor is the headstone carved.
> He died when he was twenty
> and she was practised at drawing
> him back from the brink
> cajoling in spoons of soup.
> We make little runs of understanding
> as the winter afternoon
> lights up the clothes on the rack;
> we make so many
> the glow in the grate
> almost dips below the horizon,
> but does not quite go out.
> It is a timely hint
> and I make for the door and the dark yard,
> warmed by the tea,
> talking about things quite different.
>
> David Scott[3]

In his *Critique of Pastoral Care*, Stephen Pattison provides a devastating criticism of the kind of pastoral visiting which is so ill thought through that it generates confusion, pity, or quiet resentment.[4] In a society which can be suspicious of or, in some sectors, overtly hostile to the Christian message, it will not do for representatives of the Church to assume the right to visit people in their homes or in hospital without a justifiable and clearly articulated rationale. The deeper

---

3 David Scott, 1998, *Selected Poems*, Tarset: Bloodaxe Books, p. 59.
4 Stephen Pattison, 2000, *A Critique of Pastoral Care*, London: SCM, pp. 73–9.

additional insight of David Scott's poem, however, is that having a clear rationale is not the same as having a controlling agenda. One of the most precious gifts of the pastor is often simply to stay present to the suffering of another person. So there is a difference between being purposeful and being prescriptive; and the wise pastor will preserve a sensitive space of receptivity to the spiritual possibilities which any pastoral encounter will present.

> **Practice Point**
>
> 'Loitering with intent' need not be an offence – *if* the intent is to be alert to the opportune moment of bringing spiritual, practical or emotional care.

A fourth hallmark of this kind of loving that we call pastoral care is that it takes the trouble to be effectively *informed*. Some background study is important and helpful. It is clearly a chief purpose of a book like this to provide overarching frameworks of understanding for people beginning a ministry of pastoral care. But within those frameworks, any number of more detailed issues may need to be further explored. For example, pastors engaging with elderly people will take the trouble to learn more about the problems of declining physical and mental health; or churches with a particular ministry alongside homeless people will need pastors who understand the social and political context of homelessness well enough both to engage in respectful partnerships of care and to participate in effective public advocacy.

But this is not about trying to become an expert in everything. The pastor who likes to pontificate on any topic from child rearing and marital harmony to political analysis and personal finance will soon alienate people by his arrogance. The aim of lifelong learning, as we suggested in Chapter 1, is not to fuel the pastor's egotistical self-importance but to deepen his sensitivities to the ways in which God might be at work *in a particular context*. Becoming well informed – whether it is for the eucharistic minister learning more about the needs of the housebound, or the youth worker researching the phenomenon of school refusal in teenagers – is a humble part of the ongoing discernment of a specific pastoral vocation which is called out within the wider life and responsibility of the Body of Christ (cf. Rom.12.4–8).

> **Practice Point**
>
> The pastor who is compassionate enough to take an interest in the well-being of others will be concerned enough to take an intelligent interest in the context of their lives.

A final hallmark of pastoral ministry which distinguishes it from more narrowly differentiated models of professional care is its *integrative* character. This kind of loving keeps the whole person in view and holds the whole person within a web of attentive relationships, which connect back all the way, through prayer, to the loving heart of God.

> **Practice Point**
>
> The integrative practices of prayer and theological reflection are the pastor's best protection against the fragmenting forces which would reduce his ministry to that of a mere religious technician.

A hospital chaplain tells the delightful story of the newly admitted patient who had been seen by a dozen different clinicians in one morning. The chaplain was the last to enter the woman's room. Without looking up from her magazine, the patient tossed aside her bedclothes asking 'And which bit do you want?' The chaplain was quick-witted enough to respond laughingly, 'I want all of you!'[5]

In practice, *integration* demands that the pastor should be especially attentive to the hidden aspects of individual human need and the unrecognized dimensions of a community's experience of life together. We might describe this in terms of attending to the 'soul'; but it can be tempting to reduce even this focus to a preoccupation with solely religious concerns. The presence of the pastor represents a profound respect for the whole person; his prayerful concern does not diminish his humanity by reducing his attention to a narrow compartment of issues which are labelled as 'spiritual' or 'religious'.

---

5 This story has been shared by Peter Speck in several lectures and addresses.

One of the greatest pastoral parables tells the story of the shepherd who goes out in search of his lost sheep (Luke 15.3–7). It paints a rich picture of the pastoral challenge to reintegrate individuals with themselves and with one another. In a society which tends to dehumanize us all by losing sight of vulnerable individuals on the edge of society (cf. Matt. 25.31–46) or, more subtly, losing touch with the ineffable qualities of human wholeness which are essential to preserving the 'soul' (cf. Mark 8.36) pastors pay attention to what is being lost. God asks those who are his pastors to see life whole and, for the love of God, to strive to integrate the whole of humanity within the loving embrace of his grace.

Stories of pastoral care

We have emphasized at the start of this chapter that pastoral care is always provisional and contextual. It will be instructive, then, to look back over the history of the Church to see how certain patterns of pastoral care from earlier generations have become especially influential in later times. Some of these patterns are still very much alive in our imaginations, shaping and colouring some very powerful conscious or unconscious images of the 'pastor in the mind' (see Chapter 1).

The one – and arguably the only – constant in a remarkably diverse history is the teaching and example of Jesus, the Good Shepherd, who calls his ministers to take their share in the shepherding of his people (1 Peter 5.1–4). We shall not attempt within the scope of this book to present a detailed history of practices which have evolved over more than 2,000 years. Instead, we shall present a series of snapshots in order to illustrate some of the classic themes and practices, which continue to shed light on the pastoral task today.

Koinōnia

The Greek word *koinōnia*, variously translated as 'communion' or 'fellowship' or 'community', occurs over a hundred times in the pages of the New Testament. It describes the key theological idea of participation in a common life which makes a palpable reality of pastoral care.

In the early years of the Church, *koinōnia* was a favourite term to represent the organic, living bond which unites faithful believers in Christ, drawing together the vertical and horizontal dimensions of Christian love (1 John 1.2–4). This spiritual reality is sacramentally enacted in a shared participation in the bread and the cup of communion (1 Cor. 10.16). As partakers of this intimate communion, worshippers are incorporated together as members of Christ's own Body in the world. The communion of God's people also points forward, in eschatological hope, to the fullness of life in which all people will come to participate in the unity of God's love (2 Peter 1.3–4).

For the early Church, this emphasis on the common life of fellowship was fleshed out in practical patterns of mutual care. The most radical, and probably idealized, examples of *koinōnia* care entailed a kind of primitive communism in which money and goods were held in common (Acts 2.44–45; 4.32–37). More broadly, Christians sought to be of one mind in mutual love (Phil. 2.1–4) and, especially within the household of faith, to take every opportunity to do good (Gal. 6.10).

These early evangelical ideals came to be powerfully enshrined in the classic tradition of the monastic communities which spread rapidly throughout Europe in the medieval period, providing a basic infrastructure for pastoral care over hundreds of years. These widely distributed praying communities of lay and religious, women and men, administered parishes, taught and preached, supplied food to the hungry and medicine for the sick, care for the needy and education for the poor. As centres of learning they also distilled the wisdom of Christendom and dispensed counsel and advice to spiritual and temporal leaders of the highest rank.

The common life of the monasteries was ordered by the gospel imperatives of love of God and service of neighbour. The outworking of these two poles in a spirit of deeply pastoral integration can be seen in the rhythms and disciplines of mutual accountability in prayer, work and rest laid out in the sixth-century *Rule of Saint Benedict*, which remains a touchstone for the practice of *koinōnia* to this day.

It is interesting to note how the foundational theme of *koinōnia* has resurfaced in many ecumenical deliberations in the twentieth-century Church.[6] In the face of stark divisions and impaired communion within and between the churches

---

6 See Lorelei F. Fuchs, 2008, *Koinonia and the Quest for an Ecumenical Ecclesiology*, Grand Rapids: Eerdmans.

themselves, and in response to a strident individualism in contemporary economic life, the vision of *koinōnia*, however imperfect in its embodiment, still speaks to recall Christian people to the pastoral priority of building the kind of life together where all may taste the fullness of life for which we are created.

Cura animarum

Another classic theme in the history of pastoral theology is the *cura animarum*, a Latin phrase which suggests a commitment to both the 'cure' and the 'care' of souls.[7] As Christianity began to establish itself amid the changing fortunes of the rise and fall of the Roman Empire, a concern for care and nurture of individuals and communities came to focus on solid teaching, spiritual guidance and effective discipline.

The finest exemplar of this tradition of pastoral care is Gregory the Great, whose sixth-century *Book of Pastoral Rule* is still widely read today. Gregory's counsel covers topics which today might fall under the heading of discipleship or spiritual direction. He sets a high standard of discipline and personal study for the pastor who is called to take on this 'art of arts'; and with all the psychological sophistication of one who has delved deeply into his own soul, he sets out to teach other spiritual leaders how to pay individual attention to the nurture and guidance of diverse Christian disciples.

Gregory's high ideals for the cure of souls live on in many thoughtful traditions of pastoral care today, though nowadays in a context where the role of the priest is seen in a less authoritarian and more critical light. Perhaps the greatest difference between Gregory's approach and contemporary spiritual direction would be the more muted emphasis on disobedience and sin. Although Gregory's language can sound insensitive to modern ears, it is nonetheless salutary to observe the seriousness with which sinful attitudes were challenged and conditions of spiritual health and sickness were uncompromisingly addressed.

A later development in the tradition of the *cura animarum* links the practice of pastoral care to geographically defined communities. The canonical ordering of parishes under the care of a 'curate' – that is someone authorized to exercise

---

7 For a full discussion of this tradition, see Thomas C. Oden, 1984, *The Care of Souls in the Classic Tradition*, Philadelphia: Fortress Press.

the cure of souls – became formalized in the Western Church in the early medieval period. The ideal of a pastoral presence which is rooted in community life is harder to sustain in a more mobile society, but persists as a telling witness to an abiding human sense of place and the value of local bonds of relationship.[8]

Discipline

The theme of discipline is scarcely fashionable in the modern Church; but it was regarded as an essential feature of pastoral care in earlier periods. A fourth-century sermon from Saint Augustine typifies the delicate balance which pastors were expected to uphold.

> Disturbers are to be rebuked, the low-spirited to be encouraged, the infirm to be supported, objectors confuted, the treacherous guarded against, the unskilled taught, the lazy aroused, the contentious restrained, the haughty repressed, litigants pacified, the poor relieved, the oppressed liberated, the good approved, the evil borne with, and all are to be loved.[9]

The infant Church, in an age of sometimes violent persecution, had to establish clear boundaries of behaviour for its baptized members. Those who fell short faced the discipline of the community which was maintained through firm procedures of penitence and reconciliation. The role of church leaders was central to this disciplinary authority, which drew its mandate from the charge given to Peter for the binding and loosing of sins (Matt. 16.19).

As church life became more sophisticated, so did the preoccupation with increasingly elaborate systems of moral guidance. By the medieval period, monks and priests had assembled detailed catalogues of sins and penances in the widely circulated *Penitentials*, whose moralistic excesses make depressing reading today.

The Reformation saw a reaction against both the hierarchical role of the priest and the centrality of sacramental confession. But a similar concern for moral rigour as evidence of personal salvation continued in the churches of the

---

8 For a thoughtful treatment of the pastoral importance of place, see John Inge, 2003, *A Christian Theology of Place*, Aldershot, Ashgate.

9 St Augustine. *Sermon CCIX*, quoted in John T. McNeill, 1951, *A History of the Cure of Souls*, New York: Harper and Row, p. 100.

Reformation, especially those of a Calvinist inclination. While Protestants in a more individualistic age no longer looked to the priest to administer discipline within the community, with the rise of Pietism there was a strong emphasis on mutual discipline, which came to particular prominence in the Methodist class system.

With the exception of fringe groups exercising 'heavy shepherding' it is rare to find strong patterns of discipline in the contemporary Church. In an age of moral liberalism, where church membership is seen as a matter of voluntary association, the pastoral accountability of previous generations has been privatized almost out of existence. In this context, it is not surprising that many Christians wonder if pastoral discipline – at least in the churches of the affluent Western world – has been relegated to a 'lost art'.[10] The historic tradition of Christian discipline reminds us that there is always a place for appropriate challenge within pastoral care.

Counsel

Closely allied to the theme of discipline is the ancient ministry of spiritual counsel. It is something of a modern conceit to imagine that understandings of human nature have only attained sophistication with the rise of the psychological sciences. To read Gregory's *Book of Pastoral Rule*, for example, is to be treated to the most incisive analysis of the polarities in human experience which may come to the pastor's attention. Gregory's detailed compendium shows the teacher and spiritual guide how to touch the hearts of his people 'with the same common doctrine but by distinct exhortations'.[11] Thus he distinguishes between the counsel appropriate to men and women, young and old, poor and rich. More subtly, he explores what we might term the 'winners and losers', the 'actively guilty and passively guilty', the 'protectors and competitors', the 'nonstarters and nonfinishers'.[12] Different cases are understood differently, and each is counselled accordingly.

---

10 Charles V. Gerkin, 1997, *An Introduction to Pastoral Care*, Nashville: Abingdon, p. 44.
11 St Gregory the Great, 2007, *The Book of Pastoral Rule*, New Haven: St Vladimir's Seminary Press, p. 88.
12 Summaries of Gregory's counsel drawn from Thomas C. Oden, 1984, *The Care of Souls in the Classic Tradition*, Philadelphia: Fortress Press, Chapter 4.

It would be easy to underestimate the depth of accumulated wisdom which has been handed on through traditions of spiritual counsel – and, one might add, not only within the Christian tradition – down to the present day. Later examples of particular importance include the Puritan tradition of household religious education, which has strongly influenced the Reformed Protestant movement, and the Ignatian tradition of spiritual direction, which continues to be immensely fruitful within the Catholic wings of the Church.[13] In both traditions, a seriousness of engagement with Scripture and doctrine is matched by a thoroughgoing attention to everyday relationships and responsibilities in the world.

The dawn of the modern era ushered in a powerfully humanistic approach to counselling which has grown, through the burgeoning of psychological therapies, to achieve a dominant position in popular discourse. Pastoral theologians have responded to the phenomenal rise of counselling in somewhat divergent ways. Some, especially in the United States, have eagerly embraced the new learning, promoting psychological studies to pride of place in the education of pastors for ministry in the Church. Leaning heavily on the work of theologians such as Paul Tillich, they sought to correlate the insights of modern psychology and existential philosophy with the vision of the Christian gospel, reworking traditional understandings of sin and justification in terms of guilt, anxiety and unconditional acceptance.[14]

A more measured response seeks to deconstruct the 'faith of the counsellors'[15] and to engage with some of the underlying assumptions of psychotherapy as a fundamentally humanistic enterprise. Beyond the positive and powerful agenda of regarding human beings as people of immense value and worthy of acceptance, theologians have criticized the excesses of individualism and detachment from moral concerns which place psychotherapeutic frameworks at some remove from a traditional Christian anthropology.

This critique of the therapeutic paradigm has been played out in professional rivalries between ministers who have sought formal training and accreditation

---

13 Paradigmatic examples of the Reformed tradition include the works of Richard Baxter, *The Reformed Pastor* (1655) and *A Christian Directory* (1678). The classic text of Jesuit spiritual direction remains the *Spiritual Exercises* of St Ignatius Loyola (1524).

14 Paul Tillich's landmark book of sermons, *The Courage to Be* (1952), popularized a correlation of the gospel message with the psychological concept of unconditional acceptance.

15 See Paul Halmos, 1966, *The Faith of the Counsellors: A Study in the Theory and Practice of Social Case Work and Psychotherapy*, New York: Schocken.

as 'pastoral counsellors' and those clergy and lay ministers, more typically in a British context, who have chosen to remain determinedly community-based, non-specialist and focused on the normality rather than the crises of human life. The best fruits of this sometimes unholy wrangling can be seen in the routine integration of counselling skills into training for pastoral ministry, as we shall see in the following chapter.[16]

Liberation

Some of the fiercest critiques of the psychological individualism of the modern pastoral counselling movement have come from advocates of liberation theology. A powerful line of argument insists that the pursuit of fullness of life and the alleviation of human sorrow and sin demands analysis and intervention on a socio-political scale. This goes far beyond the individual care and consolation which has often passed for traditional pastoral care. As Pattison complains, 'Psychologically-informed, individually-focussed pastoral care has become unnecessarily narrow and straitened, sometimes with consequences bordering on the disastrous.'[17]

The rise of liberation theology in the 1960s and the growing influence of feminist theology since that time have brought new and more critical issues to the forefront of pastoral theological thinking and practice.[18] The oppressive interrelationships between personal and social, economic and political, institutional and ecclesial evils have been named and exposed. A trumpet call has sounded: we know that it is no longer good enough to tackle the individual or domestic levels of human suffering without paying serious attention to the structural dimensions within which their problems arise.

Several crucial emphases have contributed to this wider understanding of the remit of pastoral care. The first is a refusal to collude with the easy separation

---

16 Further insights into the integration of counselling with spiritual care in a British context can be gleaned from the work of the Association for Pastoral and Spiritual Care and Counselling. www.apscc.org.uk

17 Stephen Pattison, 2000, *A Critique of Pastoral Care*, London: SCM, p. 82.

18 See for example Peter Selby, 1983, *Liberating God: Private Care and Public Struggle*, London: SPCK, and Zoe Bennett Moore, 2002, *Feminist Perspectives on Pastoral Theology*, Sheffield: Sheffield Academic Press.

of public from private spheres of engagement. The mass unemployment of the 1970s and 1980s in Britain, for example, drove many church leaders to question the social forces which gave rise to such large scale misery and disadvantage. Merging prophetic critique with pastoral action, churches learned to engage in critical political and economic analysis at the same time as providing individual and collective support.

A second factor is the deliberate uncovering of historic abuses which have been perpetuated under the tacit protection of powerful groups in the Church. The most shameful example which has still to be fully rectified is the collusion of church authorities in the cover-up of ministerial sexual abuse. Equally distressing, though less scandalous at a public level, is the extent to which church teaching and behaviour has contributed to a culture in which intimate domestic abuse has been tolerated and its victims silenced.

A third area of far-reaching importance is the application of critical theory to the power imbalances in the social construction of human difference. The experience of those who are *not* men, *not* white, *not* able-bodied or *not* heterosexual is being given fresh voice within the churches, not for reasons of fashionable political correctness, but out of a passionate concern to extend the solidarity and salvation of the gospel to all God's people.

This brief summary illustrates the distinctive challenge and contribution that liberationist perspectives have brought to the ongoing development of pastoral care. Not everyone will be comfortable with the issues raised by this vigorous and sometimes tough-minded approach to Christian discipleship. But it is vital for the integrity of pastoral care that questions of justice as well as mercy, truthfulness as well as kindness, should not be politely ignored. The alternative of a tame and domesticated pastoral 'niceness' is a deep affront to the radical challenge of the gospel of Jesus Christ.

Hospitality

The final motif in our survey of stories of pastoral care is one which has recently returned to prominence. Hospitality, as a building block of community, was a central feature of life in the early Church and a natural expression of the grace which believers had discovered in Jesus – welcoming one another as God in Christ had welcomed them (Rom. 15.7). But this hospitality was about more than cosy collective self-interest. The radical hospitality of early Christians reached out to the margins to draw in the poor, the needy and, most audaciously, the uncircumcised into the common life of the household of God.

It is surprising to note how little attention has been paid to hospitality in modern writing about pastoral care.[19] Yet, open-door policies of welcome to friend and stranger were essential to earlier expressions of Christian life together. The monasteries were renowned for their practice of hospitality. In an age of journeying the European orders of Hospitallers provided a welcome and protection together with medical care, ambassadorial negotiation and spiritual sustenance to countless medieval pilgrims along their way.

A theological retrieval of the practice of hospitality is a timely development in our own age of social fragmentation and cultural, as well as religious, pluralism. We live in a fearful world and one which is full of strangers. In such a context, it is not sufficient for Christians to play the bountiful host. As individuals and communities we are also called to humbly receive by sharing in other people's lives as their guests.

This rediscovery of the pastoral significance of hospitality finds many echoes in the contemporary resurgence of trinitarian theology. The mutual indwelling and hospitality which characterizes the exchange of love within the Trinity spills out through our lives in a gracious embodiment of openness one to the other. It is a matter of creating space, of making room, so that the other – who is genuinely different – can be embraced and accepted, made welcome and truly at home.

The challenge of this hospitable vision is especially keen where Christian communities engage with those of other faith traditions – both giving and receiving the treasures that have been entrusted to each to share. Henri Nouwen characterizes this dynamic as a move from hostility to hospitality, generating the kind of space where strangers can disarm their fear and defensiveness, claiming the freedom to 'sing their own songs, speak their own languages, and dance their own dances'.[20]

In our survey of pastoral practices, each lively and engaging in its own socio-historical context, we have come full circle back to the primitive Christian enactment of *koinōnia*. Where that communion is broken open to include the

---

19 Astonishingly, the authoritative *Dictionary of Pastoral Care and Counseling* (2005, ed. Hunter, Rodney, Nashville: Abingdon Press) contains no article on Hospitality.

20 Henri Nouwen, 1976, *Reaching Out*, London: HarperCollins, p. 69.

stranger as both host and guest, we enact a hopeful foretaste of the final messianic banquet in which Christ himself prepares the great heavenly feast for the healing of the nations.

The scope of pastoral care

We have seen how the hallmarks of pastoral care can be worked out in a myriad of different ways, expressed through a variety of models of ministry which embody the priorities of the Church for different times and places. It is interesting to notice the adaptability of pastoral practice and the ways in which Christians have maintained an effective pastoral presence, which is able to be embedded, quite naturalistically, within the soil of very different cultural and religious contexts.

In twenty-first-century Britain, we face fresh questions about the understanding and scope of Christian pastoral care. Two factors in particular force us to think quite carefully about the limits of the pastoral role.

In the first place, we minister in a highly differentiated society where models of 'care' have been extensively professionalized. The pastor may find herself working alongside professional carers whose understandings of their own roles are much more formalized and tightly defined. Alongside a mental health professional, say, or a social worker, how can a pastor offer a credible description of her role? It can be tempting to reduce the role to a specific area of undisputed expertise, such as 'religious care'; but we have argued already that such pigeonholing undermines the importance of seeing human life holistically and should be resisted.

The second, and related, factor is that church pastors do not have a monopoly on something called 'pastoral care'. In fact, such is the human breadth of the concept that it would be very arrogant indeed in a secularized society to claim any overriding religious rights to the exercise of pastoral gifts. What Christians do bring to the practice of pastoral care, however, is a deep anchorage in the faith and worship of a believing community which aims to work out in practice, with the help of the Holy Spirit, a profoundly theological vision of transforming love. This is a distinctive charism and a kind of ministry which is very different from, for example, the generic 'pastoral care' of a teacher in school or the very specialized professional 'care' of a psychotherapeutic counsellor.

Figure 7.1 illustrates how the broad scope of Christian pastoral care finds its core identity and significance within the life of a believing and worshipping community. The primary level of caring is the mutual care which is arguably the most important aspect of all pastoral care. It occurs where church members express their *koinōnia* in a mutual concern and hospitable care for one another and can be expressed in a multiplicity of interconnected relationships. It is the essential foundation for all other forms of pastoral work and can be seen in action week by week through informal conversations and the supportive care expressed in church meetings, children's groups and prayer gatherings.

At the centre of this rich ecology of care are those who carry a representative role within the believing and worshipping community. Usually, these ministers will have pastoral gifts and training to bring to their role; but always they will have a responsibility to enable the pastoral work of the whole community. This may be expressed, for example, through the oversight of church-sponsored groups and the work of teaching and encouragement and liturgical leadership, which sustains the informal levels of ongoing mutual care in the wider community. In most churches, the official nature of pastoral oversight is acknowledged through some form of authorization; though this may not be the exclusive preserve of ordained clergy.

Figure 7.1 An ecology of Christian pastoral care

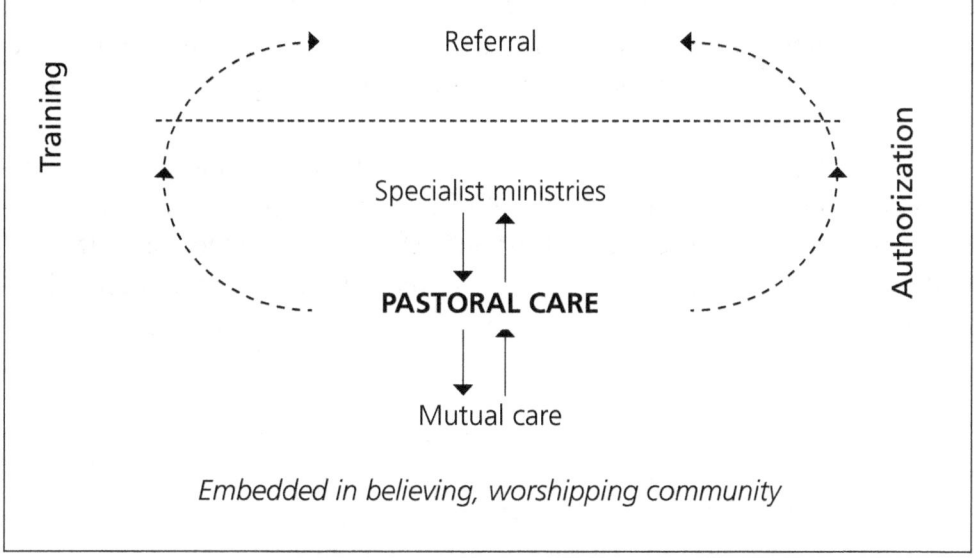

Within this relatively formal level of pastoral care, some specialist ministries will be recognized. Since not everyone can be equally skilled in all areas, it is good to foster and equip people who are gifted in particular ministries within the Body of Christ. Thus, within the local church or wider Christian networks, we might expect to find people who have specialist ministries among people at particular stages of life (younger people, for example, or the elderly), or who have developed their gifts in relation to particular groups in society (people who are unemployed, or those who are socially excluded); or those who have specialist skills in other areas such as healing, counselling or spiritual direction. Churches vary in the manner and extent to which these kinds of specialist ministries are identified, trained and authorized. But the theological principle of the unity of the Body of Christ suggests that some form of ordering and accountability through the 'sinews and ligaments' of Christian connectivity is a healthy expression of shared spiritual life together.

At the most specialist level of pastoral care, there may be a need to refer beyond the immediate networks of the church. Some important models of specialist Christian care are practised in institutional chaplaincies – for example in hospitals, universities, schools and prisons. Wherever possible it is good for these ministries to be known and affirmed in the life of local churches. Other forms of specialist care will come under the aegis of non-religious agencies – from advice services and psychotherapeutic counselling to work with the mentally disabled or those dealing with substance abuse. Although there is no sense in which the Church should seek to control or compete with secular services, there is an important ministry of prayerful interest through which pastors can affirm and celebrate the wider work of healing which is pursued throughout God's world.

Appreciating the scope of pastoral care – both in the ordinariness of much that it entails and in the extraordinariness of what it seeks to represent – is essential for the humble confidence of the Christian pastor. Her kind of loving, at the end of the day, is no more than one particular human witness to the boundless love of God from which she draws her ongoing strength and inspiration.

Keeping watch

> Keep watch over yourselves and over all the flock, of which the Holy Spirit has made you overseers, to shepherd the Church of God that he obtained with the blood of his own Son. (Acts 20.28)

Tending Christ's flock cannot be pinned down to the articulation of an influential model or the performance of an impressive protocol. The deeply personal, deeply spiritual nature of the pastor's call to care requires a particular kind of vigilance and adaptability which springs, at heart, from the pastor's own Christian integrity. It is impossible to separate the pastor from her pastoring.

We shall return to the theme of integrity in Chapter 10. At the end of this chapter, having surveyed the history of pastoral care and attempted to describe the scope of pastoral care in a contemporary British context, it will be sufficient to re-emphasize the key theological parameters of a relational understanding of human nature, an intelligent appreciation of the responsibilities of the Church and a grounded approach to mission. The humble pastor, who learns to keep watch through her own self-awareness as a Christian, together with her role-awareness as a pastor, will grow in integrity and authority in all her care for the flock.

Questions

In the light of such a diversity of historic and contemporary models, what is your own understanding of pastoral care?

Read through the summaries below. What do they emphasize that is important about pastoral care; and what do you think is missing?

- Pastoral care consists of helping acts, done by representative Christian persons, directed towards the healing, sustaining, guiding and reconciling of troubled persons in the context of ultimate concerns.[21]
- To think about pastoral theology from the feminist perspective ... requires a fundamental reorientation of the core functions of pastoral care.

---

21 William A. Clebsch and Charles R. Jaekle, 1967, *Pastoral Care in Historical Perspective*, New York: Harper Torchbooks, p. 4.

In place of or in addition to the conventional modes with which pastoral care has been routinely equated – healing, sustaining, guiding and reconciling – four other pastoral practices acquire particular importance: resisting, empowering, nurturing and liberating.[22]

- Pastoral care is surprisingly simple. It has one fundamental aim: to help people to know love, both as something to be received and as something to give. The summary of Jesus of all the Law and the Prophets in the two great Old Testament texts on love (Lev. 19.18 and Deut. 6.5) tell us … all we need to know about the tasks of ministry.[23]

Further Reading

Ballard, Paul and Stephen Pattison, 2005, *The Bible in Pastoral Practice: Readings in the Place and Function of Scripture in the Church*, London: Darton, Longman and Todd.

Beeley, Christopher A., 2012, *Leading God's People: Wisdom from the Early Church for Today*, Grand Rapids: Eerdmans.

Bennett Moore, Zoe, 2002, *Feminist Perspectives on Pastoral Theology*, Sheffield: Sheffield Academic Press.

Carr, Wesley, 1997, *Handbook of Pastoral Studies*, London: SPCK.

Clebsch, William A. and Charles R. Jaekle, 1975, *Pastoral Care in Historical Perspective*, New York: Aronson.

Deadman, Richard, Jeremy Fletcher, Janet Hudson and Stephen Oliver (eds), 1996, *Pastoral Prayers: A Resource for Pastoral Occasions*, London: Mowbray.

Evans, Gillian R., 2000, *A History of Pastoral Care*, London: Cassell.

Gerkin, Charles V., 1997, *An Introduction to Pastoral Care*, Nashville: Abingdon.

St Gregory the Great, 2007, *The Book of Pastoral Rule*, New Haven: St Vladimir's Seminary Press.

Hunsinger, Deborah van Deusen, 2006, *Pray Without Ceasing: Revitalizing Pastoral Care*, Grand Rapids: Eerdmans.

Lyall, David, 2001, *Integrity of Pastoral Care*, London: SPCK.

McNeill, John T., 1951, *A History of the Cure of Souls*, New York: Harper and Row.

Oden, Thomas C., 1983, *Pastoral Theology: Essentials of Ministry*, San Francisco: Harper.

---

22 Bonnie J. Miller McLemore, 1999, 'Feminist Theory in Pastoral Theology', in Bonnie J. McLemore and Brita L. Gill-Austern (eds), *Feminist and Womanist Pastoral Theology*, Nashville: Abingdon Press, p. 80.

23 Alastair V. Campbell, 1985, *Paid to Care?*, London: SPCK, p. 1.

Osmer, Richard R., 2008, *Practical Theology: An Introduction*, Grand Rapids: Eerdmans.
Pattison, Stephen, 2000, *A Critique of Pastoral Care*, London: SCM.
Pohl, Christine D., 1999, *Making Room: Recovering Hospitality as a Christian Tradition*, Grand Rapids: Eerdmans.
Scott, David, 1997, *Moments of Prayer*, London: SPCK.
Selby, Peter, 1983, *Liberating God: Private Care and Public Struggle*, London: SPCK.
Wells, Samuel and Sarah Coakley (eds), 2008, *Praying for England: Priestly Presence in Contemporary Culture*, London: Continuum.
Woodward, James and Stephen Pattison (eds), 2000, *The Blackwell Reader in Pastoral and Practical Theology*, Oxford: Blackwell.

8

The Art of Pastoral Conversation

Listening, Love and Language

Tending the flock involves conversation. Face to face; on the phone; email conversations; cards and messages; in the office; at the back of church; on the street; at the hospital; in the home; during a meeting; over coffee; conversations of one kind or another are as fundamental to pastoral care as breathing.

Some ministers are naturally gifted in this area. Starting up conversations and, more importantly, keeping them alive comes easily to them. There are some people who readily engage in rich and meaningful conversations. Some pastors are superb listeners; some have great warmth; some have a deeply invitational manner; some have a wonderful way with words. But most practising ministers are keenly aware of their inadequacies in this area and sensitive to the enormous burden of expectation that rides on the most humble pastoral conversation.

In this chapter, we shall take an intentional approach to conversation. However artless it may seem, we recognize that the everyday practice of conversation is a centrally important part of the pastor's work. And it is worth doing well.

Conversation is important because it symbolizes relationship. In an information culture, our society has become so caught up with the transactional content of communication that our skills and sensitivities in the richer, relational aspects of conversation have been correspondingly diminished. The distinction between mere *communication* and authentically personal *communion*

> **Over Coffee**
>
> People tell me terrible things over coffee,
> and I don't know what to do.
> If I say nothing, will they think that I don't care,
> that I am indifferent to their words.
> But if I try to speak, I am afraid
> that what I say will sound clichéd,
> debased or trite or uninformed.
> So there I sit, playing with my cup,
> stumbling, muttering, wanting very much
> to say something that will honour the immensity
> of what they say.
>
> Kathy Galloway[1]

was famously outlined by the Jewish philosopher Martin Buber. He described the depersonalizing quality of an instrumentalist approach to communication as an *I–It* relationship, in which the person is treated as a mere object rather than a genuine conversation partner. In the *I–Thou* relationship, by contrast, each person enters into a truly dialogical conversation in which a deeply spiritual exchange of mutual affirmation creates a sense of real encounter.[2]

We have seen already in this book how fundamental person-to-person encounters are to the process of human development and maturation (see Chapter 3). Human beings are conceived in encounter. From the earliest stages of being held in a mother's arms, we know that the first burbling exchanges of loving 'conversation' are foundational to the well-being of the developing child. The infant learns to talk through mimicking the speech of grown-ups; and as she finds her voice, so she finds her sense of self. No wonder loving parents delight in the first smiles, gestures and words of their growing son or daughter.

A sense of intimate encounter or communion is similarly fundamental to Christian theology. The God who has made himself present to us in Jesus Christ is committed to face-to-face encounter with human beings. In his covenant of care, he has pledged himself to our salvation, offering the fullness of his own

---

1 Kathy Galloway, 1993, *Love Burning Deep*, London: SPCK, p. 50.

2 Martin Buber, 2010, *I and Thou*, translated by R. G. Smith, Mansfield Centre, CT: Martino Publishing; original edition, 1937.

being to enter into our sin and sorrow and gifting his Spirit so that we, too, may grow into the mutual communion of Christian love.

All of this suggests that a pastoral conversation will be anything but an idle 'chat'. The representative nature of the minister symbolizes the presence of the whole Christian community. In some sense – and this can be enormously powerful for good or ill – the pastor also stands for the presence of Christ, of God. Developing the art of pastoral conversation, therefore, will require a reflective practice in relation to our conversational skills and sensitivities but even more in relation to our spirituality and its expression in compassionate availability to others.

This chapter is not intended to explore all the skills and techniques of formal counselling. The more humble aim, which is vital for pastoral integrity, is to outline a reflective approach to the conversational arts which build up Christian *koinōnia* in faith and hope and love. Let us begin, then, with the first essential of pastoral listening.

Learning to listen

> You must understand this, my beloved: let everyone be quick to listen, slow to speak. (James 1.19)

Listening comes first. This point needs to be emphasized because human beings in general, and those who are motivated to care for others in particular, are generally more inclined to focus on speaking than on listening. But listening comes first, always.

Theologically, we can think of good listening as a kind of hospitality. We are making room, emotionally and spiritually and with the gift of our attention and imagination, for the other person's thoughts and feelings to enter into our own heart and mind. To the extent that any pastor can be truly attentive, the grace of good listening takes on an almost sacramental quality. It symbolizes God's intimate presence and care. As Simone Weil observed, 'The capacity to give one's attention … is a very rare and difficult thing; it is almost a miracle; it *is* a miracle. Nearly all those who think they have this capacity do not possess it. Warmth of heart, impulsiveness, pity are not enough.'[3]

---

3 Simone Weil, 1951, *Waiting on God*, translated by E. Craufurd, London: Collins, p. 75.

Relationally, deep listening is of inestimable value. In the first place it gives an insight into the other person's world, enabling a more accurate understanding of their hopes and struggles. Second, it awakens us to the other person as worthy of respect, encouraging their maturation by attending to their growing edges of mind and spirit. The idea of *attending* is an important aspect of care. It implies a kind of intimate service, literally a 'close tending' to the person; it is a good translation of the Greek word *diakonos* which underlies the Church's ministry of the deacon. Third, good listening is an embodiment of the gospel itself: which is always attentive presence before it is wordy proclamation.

The good news for pastors is that listening skills can, to a certain extent, be learned and practised. This is not to say that the listener's essential generosity of spirit is merely a matter of technique. The willingness to be present at a deep and costly level to the pain, confusion and fear of another person, or even to enter wholeheartedly into their joys, is much more than a question of achieving the right kind of conversational competence. Nevertheless, there are particular skills and ways of listening which can be identified and improved if the pastor is to offer the very best of her attentive hospitality in tender care.

Active listening

We need to take an intentional approach to pastoral conversation. One way of practising this is to develop the skills of active listening. The word 'active' reminds us that good listening is never as easy as it sounds. To take an interest in someone at a deep level demands a focused and attentive commitment to listening. And before we even begin, it requires an honest appraisal of the appropriateness of the conversation: at this time; in this place; and with this conversation partner.

> ### Practice Point
>
> Before pursuing a pastoral conversation, it is good practice to check out:
>
> - Is the situation right?
> - Is the timing suitable?
> - Am I the appropriate person to hold this conversation?

The notion of hospitality guides us at this point. In a figurative sense, and often also in a literal sense, we need to reflect on whether we have the availability to make proper space for the conversation. Gaylord Noyce writes of the symbolic gesture of 'pulling up a chair' to signal that time is available.[4] Margaret Guenther reflects on the welcoming space that is created in her own room by a simple attention to uncluttered furnishing and the gathering of two souls in quiet conversation around a red rug on the floor.[5]

Of course, good listening is about much more than the physical arrangements of chairs and carpets. But wherever it is possible to be intentional about the protection of quiet space, undisturbed space and a space which is comfortable in terms of physical posture and eye contact, then these small details of hospitality will help to create a framework for active listening, which supports the deeper holding of heart and mind before God.

Once an appropriate ethos of listening has been created, many people will be glad to talk without further invitation. Others may need subtle encouragement. Perhaps we have noticed that they look troubled, or we are aware that there are ongoing concerns. 'Would you like to talk …?' A gentle enquiry is usually more than sufficient. Too much eagerness and curiosity is experienced as patronizing or intrusive.

Inexperienced pastors may be tempted to use a lot of questions in their eagerness to help the conversation along. But there are other more sensitive ways of prompting and facilitating which, for the person on the receiving end, feel less like an interrogation. A simple observation: 'That sounds hard …', or a tentative reflection: 'You're worried about how it's going …?' A tone of hesitant enquiry makes more space for someone to talk than a barrage of overly direct questions.

The largest, and subtlest, part of pastoral listening is always non-verbal. We convey to others the genuineness of our interest, not by earnest-sounding enquiries, but by the responsive demeanour of our eyes and face, by the quality of our closeness and our posture. Practised listeners can intuit the extent of eye contact or the level of postural 'matching' which will signal deep attentiveness and attunement. Novices have been known to ape these skills of body language, contriving to follow every twist of the mouth or bend of the head with a

---

4 Gaylord Noyce, 1981, *The Art of Pastoral Conversation*, Atlanta: John Knox Press, p. 25.

5 Margaret Guenther, 1992, *Holy Listening: The Art of Spiritual Direction*, London: Darton, Longman and Todd, p. 13.

> **Practice Points**
>
> Avoid the temptation to use too many questions:
>
> - Use questions as little as possible, but make the questions that you do ask as helpful as possible.
> - Open questions ('What …?' 'How …?') leave most room for the other person to talk freely.
> - 'Why …' questions are less helpful. They invite explanation rather than exploration, and many people find them intimidating.
> - Closed questions, which invite a 'yes' or 'no' answer, tend to discourage further exploration.
> - Some of the best 'questioning' is non-verbal. An enquiring look, if it is gentle and unthreatening, will often encourage continued reflection.

mirroring action of their own; but this is to miss the point of non-verbal communication. The significance of our own, and the other person's, body language does not lie in some detailed interpretation of every gesture but rather in the sensitive discernment which picks up and reflects back the embodied expression of deep-seated feelings. This emotional authenticity, or congruence, can never be contrived; but for good listening it must be attended to.

Michael Jacobs calls this deeper dimension 'listening to the bass line'. It takes us to the deep core of listening. Many pastoral conversations turn out to be dark and complicated, because life itself can be dark and complicated. Someone may need to talk because they are feeling confused or ambivalent; very often their emotions are difficult to express and hard for the hearer to disentangle. 'It is often because there are conflicting emotions, contradictory feelings, and opposing sets of values, that people need to find someone to talk to.'[6] Careful listening will draw out what is being said at different levels in order to help someone to explore their difficulties. 'You sound deeply disappointed at what has happened to you. Maybe also quite angry …?'

---

6 Michael Jacobs, 1996, *Swift to Hear: Facilitating Skills in Listening and Responding*, London: SPCK, p. 23.

At this point we are reminded of the costliness of genuine listening. Opening ourselves in heart and mind to the fearful tangles of a troubled person's situation, or taking into ourselves, like a pin cushion, the griefs and pains of a suffering person's long lament, will demand a level of receptivity which can only be sustained through grace. The skills of listening might help us to bear this conscientiously; but it is only through faith and hope and love that we can look to God for healing and transformation.

The shape of pastoral conversation

In an introductory book, it would be unwise to attempt to summarize the extensive skills which are deployed by trained therapists. Professional counselling interventions should only adopted by those who are appropriately qualified and supervised in this field. But it would be equally unhelpful to discount the enormous power for good in an intentional conversation with a discerning and compassionate minister. The humble pastor discovers a resource for profound emotional and spiritual transformation in the conversations of everyday pastoral encounters.

An attentive pastor offers far more than an inert sounding board. Her formation in the wisdom and spirituality of the Christian faith has shaped a wealth of experience and expectation of God's transforming grace. This experience and expectation will frame her ministry of conversation at a very deep level, enabling a humble response to the other person which is grounded in being human, being present and being good news (see Chapter 1). In a later chapter, we shall explore in more detail how the rich narratives of the gospel intersect with, and illuminate, the progress towards maturity in growing human souls (see Chapter 11). At this point, we introduce a simple model of the shape of pastoral conversations which can support and sustain such potential development.

Presence is the first essential. Striking up a conversation may not always be plain sailing; but the pastor enters into each personal encounter with quiet expectancy. If the context is right, then some opportunity to establish a listening presence will readily arise. For the experienced pastor, the social niceties of what is called 'small talk' work to pave the way for later 'soul talk' as the ground is laid for a relationship of deeper trust and availability. *Establishing presence* as the first stage of a pastoral conversation requires a light touch, plenty of patience

Figure 8.1 The shape of pastoral conversation

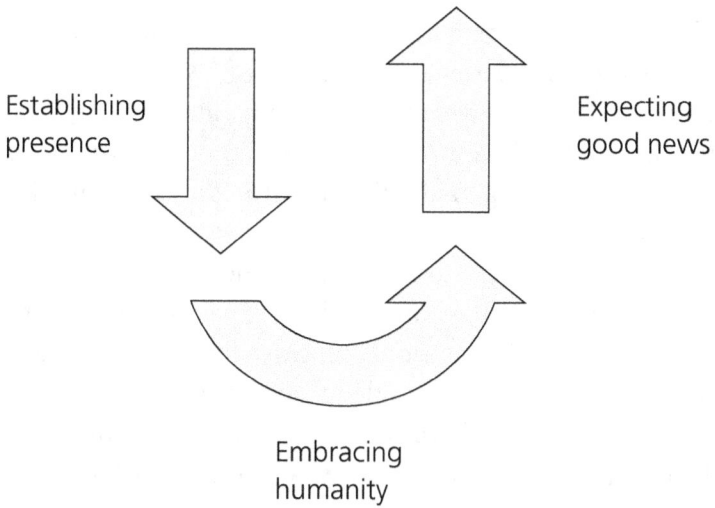

and the discipline to put aside one's own preoccupations to make room for genuine engagement.

If the context is right and a conversation begins to develop, then the quality of presence established becomes a matter of some importance. Counselling theorists speak of the three core conditions of congruence, respect and accurate communication of empathy.[7]

Congruence is a vital aspect of pastoral integrity which suggests an emotional and spiritual transparency – without facade or defensiveness or striking a pose. If the pastor is not able to be honest or at ease in her own humanity, then it is unlikely that her conversation partner will feel able to engage at any depth. Self-awareness is the key to an honest and authentic quality of presence which refuses the shortcuts of genuine engagement.

The quality of *respect* is perennially important in human relationships and especially crucial to uphold, if the conversation is in any way challenging to the pastor. It takes considerable self-awareness to maintain an unconditional attitude of respect, when the conversation seems to threaten the pastor's understanding or authority or to call her out of her comfort zone.

---

7 These three conditions have been widely developed and applied based on the principles of Rogerian person-centred counselling. See Carl A. Rogers et al., 1957, 'The necessary and sufficient conditions of therapeutic personality change', *Journal of Consulting Psychology* 21, pp. 95–103.

The third core condition of *accurate empathy* is the one which research shows to be most susceptible to training. Careful practice can build up the resources for empathic engagement by harnessing a breadth of perceptivity and imagination through reflection on our own life experience and relationships, as well as the emotional intelligence gathered from prayer and meditation, literature and the arts. It is a matter of cultivating a sensitive awareness of the inner world, with all its emotional complexities, and learning to identify and express these subtleties with precision and clarity for someone else.

Empathy is thus the skilful handmaiden to compassion, the quality of 'suffering-with' another person. Through compassion we offer a capacity to enter into the perceptual world of another person, to become sensitive to their fear or rage or tenderness or confusion. In that way we are able to travel with them into the deeper places of pain and struggle where healing needs to take place. This is the incarnational principle, indispensible for truly Christian ministry, which puts tender-heartedness at the centre of human relationships just as it is at the centre of the heart of God (Luke 6.36).

In this respect we need to understand how different the cure of souls is from the cure of the body or mind. Scientific therapies approach the challenge of healing through the powerful diagnostic processes of an *I–It* relationship. This is not the case with pastoral care, which probes the depths of sin-sickness through gentle *I–Thou* relationships of solidarity and mercy. Henri Nouwen puts the challenge of this healing compassion very clearly:

> Compassion asks us to go where it hurts, to enter into the places of pain, to share in brokenness, fear, confusion, and anguish. Compassion challenges us to cry out with those in misery, to mourn with those who are lonely, to weep with those in tears. Compassion requires us to be weak with the weak, vulnerable with the vulnerable, and powerless with the powerless. Compassion means full immersion in the condition of being human.[8]

The shape of pastoral conversation must tread the path of compassion, where two souls discover the depths together and find that Christ is present in their meeting.

---

8 Henri J. M. Nouwen, Donald McNeill and Douglas A. Morrison, 1985, *Compassion: A Reflection on the Christian Life*, New York: Image Books, p. 4.

THE ART OF PASTORAL CONVERSATION

The closing dynamics of a pastoral conversation are not unlike those of an effective liturgy (see Chapter 6): it is important that the conversation should end well. Indeed there is a sense in which no pastoral exchange is complete without a concluding blessing. Of course, this is not to suggest that a formal or priestly benediction should always be invoked; still less to recommend a clichéd 'God bless' at the end of every conversation. What the pastor communicates is a firm *expectation of good news* which shapes the ending of a conversation and supports the parting of the ways.

We can trace a rich pattern of good news in the incarnation, passion and glorification of Christ, which culminates in his leaving the disciples with the gift of the promised Advocate (translated in older versions as the 'Comforter'). Jesus' farewell discourses in the gospels emphasize the continuing grace of the Holy Spirit: his disciples will not be left comfortless (John 14.18); they will receive power (Luke 24.49); his presence will still support them (Matt. 28.20); they need not fear for the future (John 14.1); they will be reminded of the truths they need to hold on to (John 14.26); and they will be held in his peace (John 14.27).

A similar kind of pattern shapes the final phase of an effective pastoral conversation. It does not simply drift to an end. It never leaves a person pitilessly exposed. Instead, there is an intentionality about the way that a good pastor leaves the other person with spiritual resources for the future. No verbal formula will achieve this in every situation; sometimes a simple indication of future availability – a card or email contact – is most appreciated. But more often it is the unspoken reassurance of the pastor's ongoing concern which best conveys her vicarious faith and hope and love to a troubled conversation partner. In this context the warmly held hand or generous eye contact will speak volumes. Here, as at each point in the conversation, the congruence of the pastor will leave a lasting impression.

Much more could be said to elaborate on this simple template for a pastoral conversation. We shall take up the threefold dynamic once more in Chapter 11 in connection with the narrative model of interpreting human stories. At this point, we turn to focus more deeply on one of the key elements of any conversation: the gift of language.

Loving language

The pastor needs an array of micro-skills for her relational ministry; and one of the under-recognized aptitudes of the good pastor is a particularly sensitive way with words. It is curious that in the training offered for public ministry, despite paying considerable attention to the use of words in preaching and formal liturgy, relatively little critical attention is given to the impact of words in informal pastoral settings. Perhaps this is a legacy of the ancient classical traditions of education with their strong foundations in rhetoric and public debate.

A pastoral conversation is not, however, a platform for oratorical prowess. The very word 'conversation' itself (from the Latin *conversare*, to turn constantly) reminds us that it is about taking turns. A sparkling verbal display of 'warmth, wit and wisdom' which might be properly admired in public speakers is not, therefore, the first requirement for the intimate exchanges of pastoral conversation, where more measured words are ventured into a deeply attentive space of listening and mutual exploration.

The pastor, then, has to *take care with words* in a particularly delicate setting of reciprocal disclosure and unscripted eloquence. She needs a sense of how language works; but she must apply this creative understanding in the rough and ready work of live, unpredictable exchanges where impromptu responses will be wrung out in real time, sometimes from the very depths of her own being.

A word fitly spoken is like apples of gold in a setting of silver (Prov. 25.11). Like the accuracy of empathy, the quality of aptness is essential for the value of the pastor's words. Not a great deal is required. She learns that a suitable phrase will restore calm; a gentle word-play will send out ripples of delight; a perceptive analogy will evoke deep echoes of healing truth. The pastor must be like a deft poet, offering a few words that are compact and allusive, clear and precisely tuned, with the jewel-like quality of subtle sparseness.

There is nothing precious, however, about the kind of poetics crafted in the pastoral moment. The poet Euros Bowen compares his craft to the work of a man with a litter stick, who picks up bits and pieces of paper here and there along the road.[9] Something rather similar takes place in a pastoral conversation as the attending ear picks up the tone and rhythm, the register and guiding

---

9 Euros Bowen, 1993, 'Litter Stick', in *Poems*, Llandysul: Gomer, p. 15.

imagery – almost unconsciously – for the work of crafting an empathic response to another person. Locking on to affinities and working creatively with suggestive themes, the pastor-poet pieces together a unique verbal collage which will take the conversation forward in fresh directions of significance.

In the ministry of Jesus we see the same kind of linguistic give-and-take. There is a simple profundity about his use of everyday words, crafted with the wordsmith's genius into timeless questions and parables. This is an utterly down to earth, incarnational business. 'There is no "Holy Ghost" language used for matters of salvation and then a separate language for buying cabbages and cars,' writes Eugene Peterson. '"Give us this day our daily bread" and "pass the potatoes" come out of the same language pool.'[10]

For the contemporary pastor, the same unostentatious love of language serves to pick up and resonate with everyday echoes of the divine. Staying alert to metaphors, the responsive pastor will take up and play with any tasty morsel of meaning which might tickle the spiritual imagination of her conversation partner, keeping her words simple, gracious and well-seasoned with salt (cf. Col. 4.6).

An example of this kind of responsiveness comes from research into pastoral practice in a hospice setting. Rachel Stanworth collected a rich catalogue of images and metaphors that cropped up spontaneously in conversations with patients at St Christopher's Hospice in London. Many were light-hearted throwaways and flippant asides; yet these little gobbets of existential significance revealed how people were grappling with major concerns through a largely non-religious language of the spirit.[11] Learning to recognize profound themes of liminality and letting go in symbols, metaphors, silence and humour helped chaplains and others to develop deeper conversational resources for effective spiritual care.

In all this the pastor must tread softly. Half-spoken meanings may be misconstrued or clumsily interpreted; and nothing will be gained by pressing an alien agenda. So she proceeds with care, but also with humble confidence in the grace of the Holy Spirit who reveals in the midst of the moment words that cry out to be heard (cf. Luke 12.12). Like the sower with a bagful of tiny seeds, the pastor tosses out her little gems of gospel conversation along the path, trusting

---

10 Eugene H. Peterson, 2008, *Tell it Slant: A Conversation on the Language of Jesus in His Stories and Prayers*, Grand Rapids: Eerdmans, p. 11.

11 Rachel Stanworth, 2004, *Recognizing Spiritual Needs in People who are Dying*, Oxford: Oxford University Press, pp. 60ff.

that where the soil is ready and good, new life will someday spring into being (Luke 8.5–8).

Keeping the conversation going

The art of conversation makes relationships, sustains relationships, heals relationships. In the fast-paced culture of contemporary life it is therefore a vital part of the pastoral vocation to preserve the values of conversation.

Because relationships need to develop over time, it is important to cultivate an ethos – in our homes and churches, schools and institutions – which values conversation. Heije Faber reminds us that the particular subject of conversation is rarely the primary issue in pastoral relationships. If pastors are open-minded then people will discuss all kinds of things with them.[12] More important is the 'extra' dimension of a pastoral conversation: the sense that a person is left feeling that they have been heard, that someone has taken the time to ask about their lives in more than a perfunctory way. These are the qualities which leave an impact.

Such conversational values build over time. It would be unreasonable to expect that every fleeting conversation will be of immense spiritual moment. But in the ongoing intercourse of pastoral relationships, the flow of shorter or longer conversations works to knit together the organic 'sinews and ligaments' of the Body of Christ which are so essential for sustained Christian maturity (see Chapter 6).

From time to time special challenges will arise. The pastor will be faced with conversations that make her anxious, or angry. All too often a demanding conversation will present for which she is quite unprepared. These occasions are as much a test of spiritual resilience as of communicative skill; and it helps to acknowledge that the 'outcome' of such difficult conversations may not be known until some considerable time after the event. Not everything hangs on the seeming 'success' or 'failure' of today's conversation; and the humble pastor learns to entrust the most challenging, as well as the most humdrum, conversations to the mercy of God.

---

12 Heije Faber and Ebel van der Schoot, 1962, *The Art of Pastoral Conversation: Effective counselling through personal encounter*, Nashville: Abingdon, p. 168.

From an eternal perspective, the everyday small talk which sustains *koinōnia* is of no less significance than the deep conversations at times of pastoral crisis or spiritual turning point. Amid the seeming inconsequence of ordinary greetings and exchanges of news, not to mention the constant traffic of email messages and administrative exchanges, a web of incarnational grace continues to weave. This is the territory for conversational humility and, according to Eugene Peterson, it is a real creative art.

> I do not want to be misunderstood: pastoral conversation should not bound along on mindless clichés like gutter water. What I intend is that we simply be present and attentive to what is there conversationally, as respectful of the ordinary as we are of the critical. Some insights are only accessible while laughing. Others arrive only by indirection. Art is involved here. Art means that we give ourselves to the encounter, to the occasion, not condescendingly and not grudgingly but creatively.[13]

We have identified in this chapter some of the hard-won skills which sustain a high quality of pastoral conversation in everyday ministry. For most of us, there is scope for much greater attentiveness to the depth of our listening and the quality of our responding and a great richness to look forward to in developing more gracious and effective encounters from day to day. Let us keep the conversation going.

Questions

Questions for private journaling or prayerful reflection

- Can you think of an occasion when you experienced being listened to as hospitality? How did it feel to be listened to like this?
- Think of an occasion where a conversation has been especially challenging for you. Reflect on what you did and the pastoral values you hoped to embody. How might you approach a similar challenge in the future?

---

13 Eugene Peterson, 1984, 'The Ministry of Small Talk', *Leadership Today* 5(3), pp. 88–9.

Questions for group discussion

- What does it mean for you to 'listen to the bass line' in a conversation?
- What are the resources which help you to become more empathic in conversation?
- What value do you place on 'small talk'? How do you see this as part of your own practice of pastoral care?

Further Reading

Capps, Donald, 2001, *Giving Counsel: A Minister's Guidebook*, St Louis, MS: Chalice Press.

Ferder, Fran, 1986, *Words Made Flesh: Scripture, Psychology and Human Communication*, Notre Dame, IN: Ave Maria Press.

Guenther, Margaret, 1992, *Holy Listening: The Art of Spiritual Direction*, London: Darton, Longman and Todd.

Hunsinger, Deborah van Deusen, 2006, *Pray Without Ceasing: Revitalizing Pastoral Care*, Grand Rapids, Eerdmans.

Jacobs, Michael, 1993, *Still Small Voice: An Introduction to Pastoral Counselling*, London: SPCK.

Jacobs, Michael, 1996, *Swift to Hear: Facilitating Skills in Listening and Responding*, London: SPCK.

Kirkpatrick, Bill, 2005, *The Creativity of Listening: Being There, Reaching Out*, London: Darton, Longman and Todd.

Long, Anne, 1990, *Listening*, London: SPCK.

Lyall, David, 1995, *Counselling in the Pastoral and Spiritual Context*, Buckingham: Oxford University Press.

Mitton, Michael, 2004, *A Heart to Listen*, Oxford: Bible Reading Fellowship.

Pembroke, Neil, 2002, *The Art of Listening*, Grand Rapids: Eerdmans.

Ross, Alistair, 2003, *Counselling Skills for Church and Faith Community Workers*, Maidenhead: Open University Press.

Whipp, Margaret J., 2010, 'Taking Care with Words: Everyday Poetics in Christian Pastoral Care', *Practical Theology* 3 (3), pp. 341–9.

9

Boundaries and Power
The Limits of Pastoral Care

Integrity of practice is an essential ingredient of the Christian call to care. The right use of power is a central question for pastors because of the unique position with which they are entrusted. Whether ordained or lay, those who represent the care of the Church need to understand how to use their power to safeguard trust and to protect those who may be vulnerable to exploitation or abuse. This chapter explores the significance of interpersonal boundaries for pastoral theology and reflects on the complex power dynamics of caring relationships in which attention to limits becomes a vital key to ministerial integrity.

Beautiful boundaries

Boundaries are a healthy aspect of all human relationships. They present one way of recognizing and respecting our distinctive personal needs and possibilities. A good understanding of boundaries is vital for the practice of pastoral care, if we are to respect and nurture those who are entrusted to us and safeguard the vulnerable from potential harm.

A biological analogy

A natural boundary which is most intimately familiar to all human beings is the skin. Biologists call it the *integument*, a word closely related to the idea of *integrity* or personal wholeness. Like many symbols from the natural world, the skin in which we live carries a wealth of meanings – medically and sociologically, as well as emotionally and spiritually.

At the most basic level, as every child knows, 'it's the skin that keeps you in!' Marking and protecting the boundaries of the body, it is the skin that secures a fundamental sense of personal identity for each man, woman and child on the planet. But the living skin provides a far more interesting image of human boundaries than some impervious or unfeeling outer casing.

For one thing, human skin has a permeable character, allowing a subtle two-way exchange of elements with its surrounding environment. It is also exquisitely sensitive, abundantly equipped with nerve endings responsive to touch and pressure, heat, pain and position. More wonderfully, each person's skin tells a particular story, chronicling the interface between that person and their world – from the scars that speak of hurt and healing to the lines and wrinkles that trace a lifetime of laughter and loss.

This beautiful boundary of human skin defines and defends the unique biological parameters of a person's life. No wonder we treat it with such tenderness and respect.

A psychological necessity

A good sense of personal boundaries is essential for psychological health and spiritual well-being. We say that someone is 'comfortable in their own skin', when they are secure in their identity, neither excessively dependent on others nor unhealthily detached from close human relationships. The ability to set effective boundaries at the interpersonal level conveys care and respect for our own and other people's feelings, needs and values.

Because pastoral care may entail deep and delicate interactions with other people's lives, it is essential for the pastor to be attentive to her own personal boundaries as she comes into close contact with people in need.

> **Practice Points**
>
> - Do you have a prudent sense of the limits of your responsibility and concern?
> - Are you able to manage your own mental, emotional, spiritual, sexual space?
> - Can you graciously resist inappropriate demands and unwanted intrusions?
> - Are you alert to situations which resonate with your personal vulnerabilities and which may cloud your judgement?
> - Can you keep personal things personal and yet still be warm and open to others?
> - And, if you have good boundaries for yourself, can you adjust your own boundaries for the person who is weak or confused about theirs?
> - Do your boundaries need to be policed by rules and protocols, or have you developed the maturity to respond with confidence and flexibility to the needs of others?

Fuzzy edges and faithful care

Of course, very few relationships in life come with clearly defined limits and unequivocal boundaries. In the delicate field of pastoral care it would be obtrusive, and usually unhelpful, to insist on an explicit contract of mutual expectations. Indeed, it has been one of the great strengths of pastoral care in the British tradition to offer the kind of incarnational presence which weaves a flexible presence within the warp and the weft of everyday life. This naturalistic pattern of human involvement may be very different from the more self-conscious detachment adopted by, for example, a professional counsellor or social worker.

But a loosely defined style of presence means that the boundaries of pastoral care will be inherently fuzzy and can be easily confused. It may be hard for clergy, for example, to distinguish between work and socializing. Does a friendly chat about how the children are getting on at school represent a formal pastoral encounter? And what about having a drink at the local pub? It will not always be clear whether a minister is 'on duty', when people meet him in settings outside a formal church context.

Unlike many other professional carers, the pastor's pattern of meeting people may also be very elastic. The time, place, duration and frequency of seeing people will vary. An isolated email exchange or a brief word at the back of church may be as significant as an extended home visit in terms of the opportunity for pastoral engagement which it provides. But such flexibility also risks a degree of uncertainty which may pose problems for the integrity and intentionality of the relationship.

For this reason, it is important for the pastor to remain vigilant and self-aware about keeping appropriate boundaries.

Pastoral Story

Simon was still in his thirties when he came to have pastoral charge of his first church. As a new vicar, he was glad of the warm welcome shown by his churchwardens and especially appreciative of the friendship shown by one of them called Lawrence.

Lawrence and his family had many connections in the area. Lawrence was well established in practice as a solicitor and Sue, his wife, was the Deputy Head at the church school. They were both very hospitable to Simon and his family in their early days in the parish, making efforts to introduce them to key people in the neighbourhood and taking care that Simon's wife and children felt fully involved in the church and community. Simon was especially grateful when Lawrence offered him a family break at his luxury time-share lodge as a birthday present.

Things became complicated, however, when Lawrence came into conflict with his fellow churchwarden. Harsh words were exchanged at the PCC, and, after a very public display of temper, Lawrence resigned from office and wrote to Simon saying that he was leaving the church.

When Simon called round to see him, Lawrence made light of the situation, saying that his argument with the church need not affect the closeness of their personal friendship. Simon left the house, feeling confused about his role and compromised in his pastoral responsibility towards Lawrence.

Pastoral power

Confusion about boundaries is often related to naivety about the realities of power in pastoral relationships. Whether we acknowledge it or not, it is a fact that significant power is involved in the role of a minister or pastor. This power accrues from several sources that relate to the training, authorization and experience of the minister; but most of all there is a subtle numinous power which attaches to their role as a spiritual leader and representative of a faith community. Because of the symbolic nature of this representative role, even lay pastors can be surprised at the level of authority which people accord to them.

From a Christian perspective, however, the exercise of power turns out to be a deeply ambiguous business. We are taught to be acutely aware of the dark side of human power, with its propensity for corruption and manipulation, especially towards the vulnerable. Perhaps it is not surprising, then, that some Christian ministers try to distance themselves from any hierarchical expectations and to disavow the genuine spiritual power which is entrusted to them. Nobody wants their ministry to be seen as a personal power trip.

There is also the bewildering experience for ministers of changing social attitudes towards the Church and her public representatives. Clergy who might once have been looked up to in the wider community find themselves increasingly marginalized in the life of contemporary society, feeling that they have lost the respect and power which their role could once command. In this shifting social context, it is not uncommon for ministers and those who seek their care to misjudge the mysterious power which still surrounds their presence and to underestimate the complex dynamics which play out as this power pervades their pastoral relationships.

Since naivety about power is hazardous for Christian ministry, it is important for those who pastor others to develop the self-awareness and role-awareness which can embrace the realities of spiritual and institutional power with humility and transparent integrity. Underpinning this stance is a critical theological understanding that power, which finds its source and goal in God, is entrusted to human beings for the sake of loving service. We could sum this up by reflecting that pastoral power is given to be used *with* others and *for* others and never *over against* them.

Asymmetries of power

When a minister is engaged in the intimate business of pastoral care for other people, careful attention to boundaries becomes especially important because of the inequalities of power which affect the relationship – for good or for ill.

- The pastor, especially if ordained, carries the weight of public office as a representative of the Church.
- The pastor is the bearer of spiritual and moral authority.
- Much routine pastoral care involves relationships with people who are relatively powerless: the young, or the sick, or the needy, or the elderly.
- People seeking pastoral care at times of personal crisis or confusion are particularly vulnerable to the misuse of power.
- Inequalities of power are compounded by a lack of clear expectations about the role of a minister, especially for those unfamiliar with church life.
- Asymmetries of power in the pastoral relationship are multiplied when there are additional mismatches of gender, age, size or status.
- Ministers may be less alert to these asymmetries of power when a pastoral contact occurs in an unfamiliar context (for example, on holiday) or in an unfamiliar medium (for example, on-line).
- The asymmetries of power that belong to pastoral care will be complicated when a minister engages with someone in a dual relationship (for example, acting in the capacity as employer or supervisor while also offering pastoral care).

The lure of the friendship model

One of the great temptations to minimize or forget the inequality of power in the pastoral relationship, according to Richard Gula, is to treat it as if it were a friendship.

The lure of this model is understandable given the warmth of trust and intimacy in a good pastoral relationship which can, naturally, be very gratifying for the minister. It is not unusual for pastoral relationships to involve some degree of shared human experience, and it is also quite common for pastoral contacts to take place in relaxed and informal settings. For these reasons, it can be easy for the minister to slip into the easy expectations of mutual friendship, forgetting the distinctive character and responsibility that comes with the pastoral role.

But is it really so unethical for ministers to befriend those who are in their pastoral care? Might this emphasis on boundaries not lead to an unnecessary aloofness and the wrong kind of professional detachment?

It is in the grey areas of pastoral intimacy that the pastor needs to hold together both a warm heart and a clear head. A moment's honest reflection about the asymmetries of trust and self-disclosure will reveal the essential difference between a friendly pastoral relationship and a fully mutual friendship between peers. Since pastoral relationships cannot enjoy the complete equality of peer friendships or the mutual sharing and disclosure which creates the emotional bonds of an intimate friendship, it can be dangerous as well as disingenuous to confuse the true nature of the relationship. The pastor is always called to be 'friendly', but never to be casual about pretending that everyone with whom he socializes can be regarded as a 'personal friend'.

Sexuality and safeguarding

The potential for confusion and hurt carries special risks whenever sexual feelings are aroused. Pastors, like all human beings, relate to other people as a unity of mind and body, heart and soul. They are not equipped – thankfully – with armour-plated inner compartments which separate off their sexual nature from their other human capacities!

It is a sad fact of history, as we discussed in Chapter 4, that the Church has not always fostered a healthy growth of sexual maturity and integration in those who are authorized as her pastors. The lingering effects of mind–body dualism in Christian thinking, and the associated problems of overly strict patterns of sexual discipline, have all too often inculcated an atmosphere of denial and collusion in matters of personal sexuality. The resulting sexual immaturity and irresponsibility among those who are entrusted with leadership has led to some appalling scandals in the public life of the Church, across all denominations.

Attitudes have changed dramatically in the last ten years or so, under the influence of new legislation and keen public scrutiny. All major churches have now adopted explicit professional and organizational guidelines designed to safeguard people in their care and to protect those who offer ministry within the churches from unfounded accusations of improper behaviour, particularly in relation to children.

At a deeper level, however, there is less evidence that churches have grappled with the underlying challenges to personal and public integrity. An inherited culture of sexual shame and endemic secrecy needs to be challenged if ministers are to grow in the spiritual and pastoral wisdom that can model a gracious sexuality. Those who engage in pastoral care will need to reflect very carefully on the close inter-relation between sexual and spiritual dynamics, by attending to the realities of their own needs for affection and love and ensuring that they are not inappropriately pursuing sexual advantage through the intimacies of their ministerial relationships.

Integrity in these areas is not easy. The strength of sexual feelings can confuse or cloud the judgement even for strong Christians and experienced ministers. It is for this reason that wise patterns of personal support and supervision are recommended; and further consideration of these practical resources will be taken up in the next chapter.

Off limits – respecting boundaries of talk, touch and time

We have identified as a central problem the fact that the boundaries of pastoral practice may be uncertain or confusing. And in this challenging context, one clear precept needs to be emphasized above all.

> ### Practice Point
>
> In the practice of pastoral care, it is the minister who bears the chief responsibility for setting, communicating and maintaining appropriate boundaries.

Trust is indispensable for effective pastoral care – both for the sake of the individuals concerned and for the reputation of Christian communities, which seek to witness to the faithful love of God. Those who are authorized by the Church to act as pastors, whether ordained or lay, must therefore respect the greatness of the trust which is committed to them and recognize the responsibility that lies with them to attend to the wisdom of boundaries. The right use of power demands that the burden of this responsibility for respecting boundaries falls upon the person with greater power.

The complexity and flexibility of pastoral practice means that generalized prescriptions about boundaries will, however, rarely be helpful. It is more important for ministers to develop a critical awareness of the significance of boundaries in their own everyday interactions. With this in mind, let us now explore some of the limits of pastoral behaviour in relation to the common problem areas of talk, touch and time.

Careless talk

There was a famous slogan in Second World War publicity: 'Careless talk costs lives'. One propaganda poster showed two military men engaged in conversation on a bus behind a couple of middle-aged civilian women; the caption read, 'You never know who's listening!' Careless talk in Christian ministry may not cost lives, but it can seriously tarnish the reputation of the church as a community of love and respect.

Consider some of the following examples of pastoral carelessness.

- A youth worker jokes with friends on a social networking site about his holiday alcohol intake.
- A church leader asks other ministers to join in prayer for a colleague who is undergoing marital difficulties.
- A vicar is overheard by lay members of the deanery synod loudly criticizing senior members of diocesan staff.
- A pastor shares sexually suggestive jokes and double entendres in team meetings.
- A local preacher uses a thinly veiled pastoral incident as a sermon illustration.
- A minister's wife enjoys frequent phone calls with a friend who likes to 'share a good gossip'.

Traditionally, the Church has observed a major pastoral boundary in the so-called 'seal of the confessional', which protects a strict level of confidentiality for penitents making a sacramental confession to an ordained priest. Considerable legal and ethical debate takes place as to whether any exceptions to this absolute rule of confidentiality should be contemplated; for example, when a crime of violence is confessed, which prompts a dilemma about protecting the wider public interest.

Far more common, however, and arguably more serious, are those everyday incursions of privacy where ministers fail to respect the personal information that is shared with them beyond the explicit safeguards of formal, or sacramental, confidentiality. Of course, not everything that is shared in a pastoral conversation can or should be regarded as confidential, but without the benefit of clearly articulated limits to confidentiality it is important that ministers learn to exercise a high level of self-discipline in relation to material that could hurt or embarrass someone in their care.

Practice Points

Richard Gula recommends the following rules of thumb for pastoral confidentiality.[1]

- The presumption is always in favour of keeping the confidence of a pastoral relationship.
- The more formal the context in which communication is exchanged, the weightier is the obligation to confidentiality.
- We should take necessary steps to ensure confidentiality by seeing that offices are properly soundproof, records are secure, and staff members are informed of their duty in matters of confidentiality.
- We should communicate our understanding of the limits of confidentiality early in the pastoral relationship, so that the other will know whose agent we are, how much we can share with others and under what circumstances we will make disclosures.

---

1 Richard M. Gula, 1996, *Ethics in Pastoral Ministry*, New York: Paulist Press, pp. 140–1.

- Outside the sacramental forum, we should not offer a blanket promise of confidentiality, since there are some things we might have to disclose for the sake of protecting the well-being of others, such as child abuse.
- Before promising confidentiality, it is better to hear what we are being asked to keep a secret.
- Confidential information should not be shared without the permission of the one who has disclosed the information.
- If we must override the duty to confidentiality, we should make a reasonable effort to elicit voluntary disclosure. If we must disclose, we should tell only those who need to know and then only what they need to know to protect another from serious harm.
- We should know the laws concerning religious privilege in our jurisdiction.
- We should not participate in gossip or presume the truth of another's opinion without establishing its foundation.

The epistle of James has some searching things to say about the ethics of speech (James 1.19–26; 3.1–11), addressed particularly to those who have responsibility in the church, and from whom high standards of integrity are rightly expected. The wise pastor who respects boundaries of talk will be sensitive not only to issues of privacy and confidentiality but will also, more broadly, pay attention to questions of time and place, tone and language, in every kind of pastoral interaction – and most especially where those who are young or vulnerable are concerned.

Dubious touch

The use of touch in pastoral encounters can be a source of profound healing, as well as enormous anxiety. 'To touch, or not to touch,' is one of the most frequent dilemmas raised by people beginning pastoral ministry. Most of us are acutely aware of the defensive climate created by current legislation designed for the protection of children and vulnerable adults. Yet, at the same time, we cannot deny those deep human instincts which long to reach out to others – to affirm, to encourage, to show care – through the simplest emotional expression of all, a personal touch.

A pastoral warrant for touching is readily found in the ministry of Jesus. His unique authority and compassion are often most evident in his readiness to cross the boundaries of religious convention to touch a person in need. We recall, for example, the stories of the unclean leper (Matt. 8.2) or the haemorrhaging woman in (Luke 8.45). In the continuing history of the Church, forms of touch, often highly ritualized, have been adopted as ways of heightening significant elements of Christian ministry – from the exchange of peace in a weekly Communion service to the anointing with oil for someone facing serious illness.

Yet, we need to be cautious. There is sufficient evidence of the abuse of touch in the intimate contexts of ministry to expose any easy presumptions of benign pastoral intention as dangerously disingenuous. We also need to be alert to the widely differing norms of touch observed by people who have been brought up in different cultures or whose experience of touch has been coloured by disability, gender or previous exploitation. Because of the imbalance of power in pastoral relationships, it is never sufficient for a minister to trust in his or her own good intentions as a basis for infallible discernment in this area.

How then can we steer a middle course between the cold detachment of those who never dare to touch for fear of being misunderstood, and the careless liberty of those who are so confident of their own blamelessness that it never occurs to them that their shoulder-crushing hugs might be experienced as intrusive or patronizing to someone who cannot share their tactile enthusiasm?

Sensitivity, caution and transparency, and above all a willingness to question one's own motives, are the chief safeguards which someone entrusted with pastoral care must observe in relation to the gift of touch.

Practice Points

- Touch must always be consensual. It may be sensitively offered, but never imposed.
- To avoid misunderstanding, gestures of touch should normally be offered only in publicly visible situations.
- Touching of a sexual nature is unethical, without exception.

Precious time

Time pressure is one of the most frequent problems voiced by ministers, and is a major contributor to clergy stress. Unlike some of the other areas of boundary control that we have considered, the protection of time is usually viewed from the perspective of safeguarding ministers from the relentlessness of other people's demands and expectations. Time alone, time to think, time for family and friends, time for prayer, time to relax, are all vital for a healthy ministry; yet, the pressure to be continually available can bear in on a pastor's soul with deadly results.

Once again, we are faced with the difficulties of a loosely bounded role. What is the difference between working time and personal time for a minister who works from her own home? And how sharply can anyone distinguish between the demands and the delights of a role which involves so many activities that other people pursue in their leisure time? It is not surprising, then, that clergy can feel diffident about asserting their need for regular time off and hesitant about communicating clearly the need for proper boundaries of time which are vital for effective pastoral care.

Sometimes, of course, the boot is on the other foot and it is the full-time 'professionals' in ministry who take for granted the willing availability of voluntary workers to keep the wheels of church life turning. Respect for reasonable boundaries of commitment should raise questions, for instance, about the need to hold meetings which go on late into the evening, or the expectation for lay officers of the church to shoulder heavy responsibilities year after year without a break.

More often, though, it is the full-time pastor who feels besieged by the seemingly endless demands of ministry and unable to set limits on the time and energy expended on their public role. Many pastors act as a magnet for people in trouble and can find themselves unreasonably burdened, when people with a poorly developed sense of their own boundaries latch on to the resources of strength and kindness that they perceive to be endlessly available in the church.

Caring for boundaries is not an optional extra for a minister who wants to remain present to her role with sufficient physical, emotional and spiritual energy for the long haul. This discipline begins with self-awareness and an honest recognition of the motives and priorities which drive the hamster-wheel of busyness. To sustain this inner attentiveness, the wise pastor will cultivate tactics of gracious withdrawal to curb her overinvolvement in the lives of others.

Bishop Stephen Cottrell has drawn attention to Jesus' practice of 'radical unavailability' in the midst of a busy ministry. He recalls Mark 1.35–38, where Jesus goes out early in the morning to pray. When Peter tells him accusingly that 'everyone is looking for you', Jesus does not return to the crowds, but moves on to a new focus in line with his God-given mission. Similarly for pastors today, we need times when we are unavailable, when the answering machine is switched on and the computer is switched off. The pastor with good boundaries has the wisdom to care appropriately through both availability and unavailability, and, to adopt Niebuhr's proverb, the wisdom to know the difference.

Dancing on the edge

In this chapter, we have insisted on the wisdom of boundaries for the faithful practice of Christian pastoral care. At a fundamental level, secure boundaries are vital for setting the safe limits within which people can function as human beings and flourish as spiritual creatures. Good boundaries in ministry preserve a hospitable spaciousness within which others can open up their needs and concerns in the assurance that they will find trustworthy support and care.

Yet, the notion of boundaries can also carry negative associations. The walls that protect may sometimes work to divide or exclude. It is for this reason that the ministry of Jesus has been portrayed in terms of breaking down walls of hostility between people and ultimately between human beings and God.

One of the paradoxes of Christian ministry is that the pastor will find herself dancing on the edge of many boundaries. She dares to come close to people whom others choose to shun. She is unafraid to speak out in the face of collusion, dishonesty and injustice. She is called to venture into the dark corners of the world, seeking out the lonely, the indifferent and the lost to connect them once more with community. The pastor is placed on the boundaries between the hopes and fears of the Church, between the life and death of her people, between the everyday business of living and the ultimate glory of heaven. Most of all, she must dwell on the borders of the holy, where the deep mysteries of God may be fathomed through prayer and silence, through worship and love.

There can be no easy prescriptions for the kind of spiritual poise which such a calling demands. While guidelines and protocols can provide valuable frameworks for the practical outworking of safe and professional relationships, the deeper cultivation of a mature character with wise discernment and moral sensitivity are matters of ongoing spiritual integrity in the life of every pastor. As an introduction to this far-reaching agenda, this chapter has identified some of the important dynamics of ministry which will merit constant vigilance and care.

Questions

Referring back to the story of Simon and Lawrence and reflecting on your own experience of giving and receiving pastoral care, consider the following questions.

- In what ways might a minister's emerging friendship with someone in their care be a factor in clouding their judgement?
- Do Christian pastors face different dilemmas in relation to boundaries from other people working in caring professions?
- Why is it so hard to think clearly about power in the exercise of Christian ministry? Have you encountered any difficulties as a result?
- What kinds of boundaries are particularly slippery in the contexts of pastoral care with which you are most familiar?

Further Reading

Cottrell, Stephen, 2007, *Do Nothing to Change Your Life*, London: Church House Publishing.
Greenwood, Robin and Hugh Burgess, 2005, *Power*, London: SPCK.
Gula, Richard M., 1996, *Ethics in Pastoral Ministry*, New York: Paulist Press.
Kearsley, Roy, 2008, *Church, Community and Power*, Farnham: Ashgate.
Litchfield, Kate, 2006, *Tend My Flock: Sustaining Good Pastoral Care*, Norwich: Canterbury Press.
Lynch, Gordon, 2002, *Pastoral Care and Counselling*, London: Sage.

All pastors engaged in authorized ministry on behalf of a Christian church should be familiar with the current good practice guidelines published by their own denomination. See, for example, the following recent reports, which are all available on-line.

Baptist Union, *Safe to Grow (guidelines for work with children and young people)*, 2008.
Church of England, *Guidelines for the Professional Conduct of the Clergy*, 2003.
Church of England, *Protecting all God's Children*, 2010.
Methodist Church, *Methodist Safeguarding Handbook*, 2010.
Methodist Church, *With Integrity and Skill (confidentiality guidelines)*, 2008.
Roman Catholic Church, *Catholic Safeguarding Manual*, 2011.
United Reformed Church, *Good Practice – Safeguarding Children and Young People in the Church*, 2004.

10

Serpents and Doves

Integrity and Good Practice in Pastoral Care

The theme of personal integrity is inseparable from considerations of good practice in pastoral care because of the normative character of the pastoral role. That is to say that in order to *act like* a good pastor, it is important to *be* a good pastor.

In this chapter we shall explore these themes in more detail, exposing some of the unavoidable complexities which can bedevil the pastoral role. We should be alerted by the warning Jesus gave to his own disciples that this is not always easy territory to negotiate: 'Be wise as serpents and innocent as doves' (Matt. 10.16). For pastors who relate to people at times of vulnerability, the fine line between the integrity of a generous heart and the naivety of an innocent abroad can be especially hard to discern.

Starting with integrity

Integrity is an indispensable mark of trust for those charged with representing the covenantal care of God to his people. It can never be taken for granted, however, either as a quality in an individual, or in the quality of care which is offered within a team. Sadly, we know from experience that once ministerial integrity has been lost the heavy burden of public expectation means that it can be extremely difficult to restore.

The inner disposition of integrity is described in the Scriptures as 'uprightness of heart' (cf. Ps. 78.72). It reflects a deep-seated unity between belief and action, motivation and practice, which is recognized by others as a kind of straightforwardness of purpose which is 'without guile' (cf. John 1.47). 'To possess integrity is to be incapable of compromising that which we believe to be true,' writes Alastair Campbell. 'To possess integrity is to have a kind of inner strength which prevents us from bending to the influence of what is thought expedient, or fashionable, or calculated to win praise; it is to be consistent and utterly trustworthy because of a constancy of purpose.'[1]

But perhaps this is setting the bar too high? The idea that pastors could be entirely free from self-interest or self-deception seems a very lofty ideal which few would dare to claim for themselves. Perhaps it is more important for each pastor to be sensitive to her own humanity, aware of her mixed motives and sincerely committed to the transparency and growing spiritual maturity, which sifts out the wheat from the dross. This requires a measure of courage and honesty to face up to parts of ourselves that may be anxious, competitive or hungry for affirmation.

Seen in this light, we might say that the kind of integrity needed for pastoral care is more about wholeness than perfection. Understanding integrity as personal integration returns us to the central importance of self-awareness, or what Campbell describes as the ability 'to retain or regain contact with the lost and repudiated aspects of ourselves'.[2] This must be a lifelong task, as the business of caring for others will gradually expose some of the more complicated aspects of our own inner world. Neil Pembroke describes the challenge for pastors in terms of coming to a mature integration with our own community of 'subselves', so that we do not inadvertently bring about damage to others or ourselves.

> In a particular individual ... one might find a loving self, an aggressive self, a fearful self, a controlling self, and a clumsy self, to name just a few of the possibilities ... If we have subselves that cause damage to self and others ... we need to work on mitigating their destructive tendencies.[3]

---

1 Alastair V. Campbell, 1986, *Rediscovering Pastoral Care*, 2nd ed., London: Darton, Longman and Todd, p. 12.

2 Campbell, *Rediscovering Pastoral Care*, p. 14.

3 Neil Pembroke, 2007, *Moving Toward Spiritual Maturity: Psychological, Contemplative and Moral Challenges in Christian Living*, Binghamton: The Haworth Press, p. 3.

In pastoral ministry, integrity must embrace both the practice of the role and the person who inhabits that role. It demands maturity of heart, therefore, as well as transparency of purpose.

> **Pastoral Story**
>
> Tracey is a Methodist deacon based on an outer estate of a large city. She is a single woman living alone in a large manse, which she shares from time to time with temporary lodgers.
>
> Tracey has a deep sense of servant ministry, feeling herself called to be alongside the marginalized in humble presence and positive action for social transformation. Not all her ministerial colleagues find it easy to relate to her 'edgy' view of ministry. But Tracey's own story of finding faith in the midst of personal hardship and breakdown is what galvanizes her to reach out to others whose lives are in fear and turmoil.
>
> In the last month, Tracey has come under increasing pressure from her relationship with a longstanding house-guest, Kimberley. Kimberley had been invited to stay at the manse for a couple of weeks in the wake of an episode of domestic violence. Three months later Kimberley is abusing Tracey's hospitality by trashing the living areas and disrupting home group meetings with outbursts of angry shouting.
>
> Tracey is afraid to challenge Kimberley and asks her superintendent to intervene. Reflecting on a complex pastoral dilemma, the superintendent is concerned at Tracey's naive approach to Christian hospitality. Together they reflect on why Tracey might have become overinvolved in caring for Kimberley, asking what kind of 'tough love' could be the best expression of good news in this context.

Great expectations

An essential factor in pastoral integrity is the ability to reflect on the relationship between the personal self and the role.

Figure 10.1 The effect of the role on the personal self

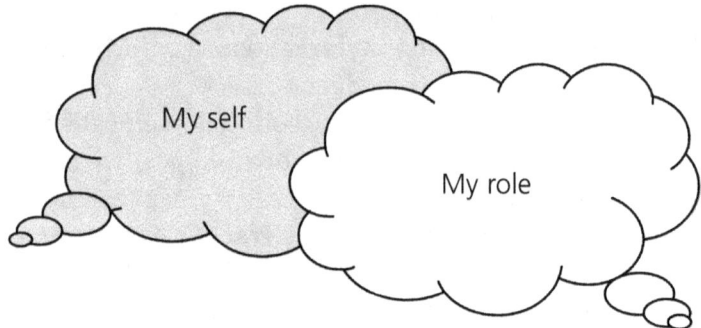

The idea of a *role*, in the context of ministry, is a powerful social construct. It reflects the expectations which other people hold, and which the minister herself holds, about the beliefs and values, behaviour and practice, attitudes and feelings, knowledge and skills which are appropriate to someone in a pastoral position. In contrast to other professional groups, ministers often find that their role is only vaguely defined in formal documents, leaving a great deal of unspoken expectations, which are open to widely different interpretations.

A great deal of uncertainty revolves around the representative nature of the role. The pastor is not seen merely as someone who performs pastoral functions. Vitally, she is also regarded as someone who represents the ministry of the Church; and at a very deep and often inchoate level, she is also seen as someone who represents the immanent presence of God. In this sense, we can think of a pastor as being a living symbol for others in a role which, rather like a lightning conductor, may be charged with a great deal of emotional and spiritual electricity.

Recognizing the intensity of this symbolic role is crucially important for the pastor's integrity, if it is not to overwhelm or destabilize her personal self and her close relationships. Alastair Campbell warns that the demand to be a living symbol

> elevates the individual to an unrealistic, and often intolerable, 'heroic' level. The weakness and evident humanity of the practitioner cannot be admitted

for fear of betraying the ideal. The result is often at great cost to the personal integrity, family life and emotional health of the representative person who attempts to meet every expectation.[4]

In the evolving interplay of self-awareness and role-awareness, the pastor needs to be alert to the unconscious expression of what psychoanalysts call 'transference'. In broad terms, this relates to the strong attitudes and intense emotions – whether positive or negative – which circle around people in ministry, and especially clergy. The intensity of these dynamics can be bewildering to new pastors who are unused to being the focus of exaggerated and often conflicting responses. Some people will think they are absolutely marvellous, while others will be sneering, dismissive or endlessly critical!

Managing these expectations is an important aspect of good pastoral care, but no one should underestimate the potential strain involved. The most important insight is to be aware of the intensity of both positive and negative projections and stereotypes in order that any distortions can be handled with a degree of patience and detachment.

More difficult for most ministers to negotiate is the complicated territory where other people's intense reactions trigger areas of difficulty in their own inner life. The emotional and practical challenges of this kind of complex overlap can be seen in Tracey's story where elements of her own background had made her psychologically vulnerable to the unreasonable behaviour being acted out by a guest in her home.

Figure 10.2 The effect of the personal self on the role

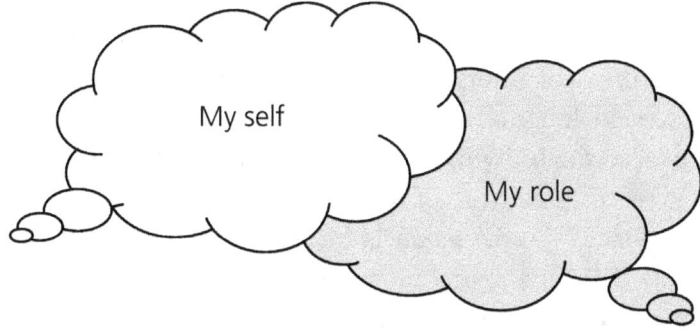

---

4 Alastair V. Campbell, 1985, *Paid to Care? The Limits of Professionalism in Pastoral Care*, London: SPCK, p. 24.

Hugh Eadie has identified a cluster of issues for pastors who are motivated for ministry by the attributes of the so-called 'helping personality'.[5] Like any other profile, this personality has characteristics which are both positive and negative: what matters, therefore, is the self-awareness to relate constructively in the role. 'Helping' persons are strongly motivated by high expectations of themselves and an altruistic desire to care and take responsibility for others. However, there may be associated characteristics which give rise to difficulties if the 'helping' person does not also attend to their own needs for love and self-esteem. While generalizations are wrong and unhelpful for any type of personality, it is important to recognize that people who are drawn to caring roles may not always find it easy to receive proper care for themselves.

With such insights in mind, the wise pastor learns in the midst of caring for others to attend to her own fullness of life. She will refuse to go along with the distorted stereotypes which deny that pastors ever get angry, feel sexual desire or experience times of depression and doubt. Instead, keeping a healthy sense of perspective and enjoyment in life, she will keep company with the kind of friends and advisors who can help her to put aside the persona or mask of ministry in order to stay in touch with the deep truths of her own inner life before God.

For Tracey, it was a conversation with her superintendent which helped her to gain a deeper perspective on her pastoral relationships and to work out how to assert her personal boundaries in ministry with greater integrity.

Supervision and pastoral care

We have emphasized that integrity is a vital personal quality for pastors, but it would be misleading to think of ministerial integrity solely in terms of the individual. As Christians, we belong to the Body of Christ, and we need all the resources of wisdom and accountability which the Spirit gives to the Church to help us grow deeper in grace and maturity of care.

In pastoral care, some form of supervision is increasingly recognized as a ministerial priority. While different churches provide structures which vary according to their historic understandings of ministry, a classic biblical model

---

5 Hugh Eadie, 1975, 'The Helping Personality', *Contact* 49, pp. 2–17.

of 'oversight' underpins a broad understanding of the importance of this role (cf. Acts 20.28; 1 Tim. 3.2). Many contemporary approaches to supervision have been helpfully informed by practices drawn from caring professions such as social work and counselling, but Christians must also look to the deep roots of their own tradition for a theological account of its significance.

Figure 10.3 The supervision continuum

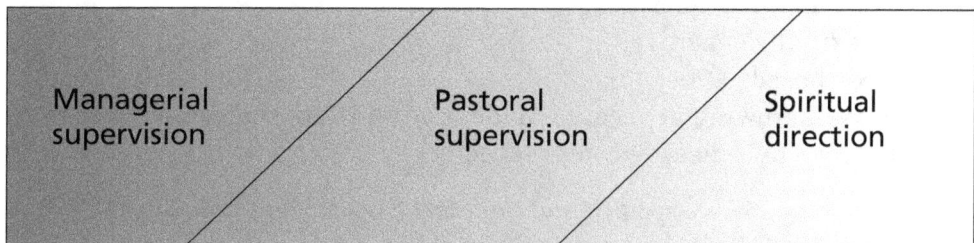

Christian pastors may be familiar with several models of role accountability, some of which overlap with the provision of pastoral supervision (Figure 10.3). At one end of this continuum is managerial supervision with its emphasis on organizational tasks and performance. Although some effective pastoral supervision will take place in this context, the hierarchical power relationships between employer and employee (whether salaried or not) may limit the degree of openness which is important for deeper levels of personal growth and exploration. At the other end of the continuum is the confidential relationship of spiritual direction which is properly focused on personal integrity and spiritual growth. While elements of pastoral supervision can be addressed in such an intimate relationship, it is not necessarily the most appropriate context within which to explore the detailed development of a pastoral role.

Whoever is identified as the most appropriate supervisor, it is helpful to define the boundaries of supervision as clearly as possible so that the pastor – especially in the early stages of ministry – can be confident that her development in ministry is being taken seriously. A church that is sloppy or idiosyncratic about providing this supervision, according to Alan Wilson, is failing to fulfil its divine calling to care.[6]

---

6 Alan Wilson, 1999, *Promoting Wholeness: An Outline of Ministerial Supervision*, Diocese of Oxford, p. 5.

> **Practice Points**
>
> Pastoral supervision is:
>
> - a regular, planned, intentional and boundaried space;
> - a relationship characterized by trust, confidentiality, support and openness;
> - spiritually / theologically rich;
> - psychologically informed;
> - contextually sensitive;
> - praxis based;
> - a way of growing in vocational identity and pastoral competence;
> - attentive to issues of good practice.
>
> Association of Pastoral Supervisors and Educators[7]

The agenda for times of supervision will vary according to the context of pastoral care and the experience of the pastor. Wilson identifies four functions which require routine attention in these sessions: support, education, management and mediation.[8] Within a broader educative relationship, we should add that the core practice of theological reflection is also important to cultivate.

Support

Good support is absolutely essential to pastoral care. No one can give good care to other people if they are feeling anxious, undermined or overwhelmed in their own position. Recognizing the kind of overextension which may be typical for the 'helping' personality, it is vital for pastors themselves and those who oversee them to ensure that effective emotional and practical support is in place.

A first essential is that the pastor should feel accepted and validated in her role. This is not something to take for granted, especially when a new position

---

7 Association of Pastoral Supervisors and Educators, 2010. From Appendix A to the Constitution. http://www.pastoralsupervision.org.uk/3.html [Date accessed 1 September 2012].

8 Wilson, *Promoting Wholeness*, pp. 29–40.

has been created, or where the pastor is at risk of being undermined by others on account of her lay status, or because of her race, gender or churchmanship. Anything that puts the pastor in doubt about the validity of her role will put unreasonable strain on her sense of security and potentially cripple her ministry.

The case of Tracey illustrates a second essential of attending to physical and emotional security. It is particularly important that the pastor feels safe enough in the supervisory relationship to air her feelings freely and honestly. Of course, this is not just a matter of letting off steam, as one might do with a good friend or partner. The supervisor aims to create a trusting environment in which it is possible to reflect critically on pastoral failures as well as successes without feeling threatened.

Education

There is always more to learn in the field of pastoral care. But giving and receiving constructive feedback is a delicate matter which requires care and respect between two adults who are both lifelong learners in the school of Christ.

Good educational supervision gives everyone permission to learn from their mistakes. If both parties are confident in the relationship, then there is no need for competitive behaviour to get in the way. The supervisor who is secure in his own educational role can say, for example, 'I know that this is an area which I struggle with too. Please feel free to learn from my mistakes!' Such an approach will go a long way to defuse resentment or frustration, modelling a healthy approach to limitations in knowledge and pastoral skill.

A good supervisor will be generous and open in sharing his own knowledge and expertise. Far more importantly, he will foster a reflective culture of mutual learning as a powerfully enabling basis for improved pastoral practice.

Reflection

We have emphasized throughout this book the strongly theological basis for Christian pastoral care. Good supervision will engage with this theological foundation through regular attention to reflective practice.

This means taking time to probe more deeply the connections between faith and ministry. In practice it requires disciplined reflection on experience, which is always better pursued in conversation, so that the integrity of what is intended and achieved can be explored in real depth in the light of our understanding of the call of the gospel.

> **Practice Point**
>
> A *critical incident* is an event which prompts deep reflection. It gives us pause for thought. Analysing a critical incident with a supervisor and/or peers is a simple and effective form of theological reflection.
>
> - Describe the situation fully, noting carefully all relevant factors. Who was involved? Where did it take place? What was the background to this incident?
> - What made the incident critical for you?
> - Apply your theoretical frameworks (for example, from pastoral psychology) to probe more deeply what is going on in this situation.
> - Ask yourself 'Where is God?' in this situation. Use your imagination and your knowledge of the scriptures to make connections with the great theological themes of creation, redemption and fullness of life.
> - Gather up your insights for future practice. What have you learned about God? What have you learned about your ministry? What have you learned about yourself?

It is beyond the scope of this book to go into detail about models of theological reflection, and a number of excellent introductions are readily available. Suffice it to say that any simple method of reflection which enables thorough exploration of critical incidents can be a very helpful tool for supervision. It provides a clear framework for learning from experience which is more disciplined and more intentional than simply mulling things over out loud. Performed well, it will foster deeper insight and integration for both the pastor and her supervisor, stimulating both to grow in wisdom and creativity for their shared vocation.

Tracey's extended reflection on her relationship with Kimberley uncovered some profound questions about the source of her confidence in ministry. She learned that following Christ was not a matter of giving away her need for self-respect and that true compassion could sometimes be expressed through appropriate challenge and assertiveness. More than anything, she learned from her Superintendent that through honest prayer and reflection she could bring her inexperience into the open without fear, trusting that God would guide and strengthen her ministry through the support and encouragement of others.

Management

We have already noted some of the overlaps between managerial supervision and pastoral supervision. It will be important, therefore, in view of the power relationships involved, for the pastor and her supervisor to be quite clear about the managerial dimensions of the role. Any confusion about the supervisor's authority – for example as someone who will write references or reports – will only breed confusion and insecurity, undermining the potential for learning and growth.

Clarity of communication, in both directions, is essential in this area. It is not unknown for pastors with considerable life experience to find themselves accountable to someone in the church who is relatively new to management responsibilities. In this situation, a diplomatic approach to 'managing up' can help both parties to become clearer about their expectations.

Many clergy have understandable and deep misgivings about what is called 'managerialism', fearing the attempt to make the church function like a secular organization. No one likes the kind of overinflated bureaucracy which formalizes friendly relationships and stifles creativity. As long as the aims of supervision are met and the responsibilities of management are fulfilled, then there is nothing wrong with a friendly informality. But, as Alan Wilson points out, 'the sober truth is that informal styles require *more* clarity and a *higher* degree of personal organization from both supervisor and supervisee'.[9]

With this warning in mind, both pastor and supervisor need to respect such essential, if unexciting, managerial matters of proper pastoral administration, data protection and adherence to safe working practices. Cutting corners in these areas of organizational detail is a serious abrogation of pastoral responsibility.

---

9 Wilson, *Promoting Wholeness*, p. 13.

Mediation

Within the overall remit of supervision, Alan Wilson includes a mediatory function in order to emphasize the web of relationships within which pastoral practice takes place. The integrity of any individual pastor is organically bound up within the quality of these relationships with other team members, office holders and outside people and agencies. It is part of the function of good supervision, therefore, to foster and to oversee the development of healthy relational networks.

Much of this mediatory role will be positive, directed towards encouragement and the forging of introductions where necessary. Sometimes, however, an element of conflict will have to be negotiated and the clarity of supervisory oversight will be of enormous importance in minimizing any damage to overall confidence in a ministry team. Most of all, it will be helpful for everyone if the supervisor himself encourages healthy patterns of communication, modelling the kind of attitudes and procedures which build mutual loyalty within the pastoral team.

The shadow of abuse

There is a critical role for supervision in the prevention of ministerial abuse. The history of pastoral care reveals a dark and ugly shadow side of caring which can take the form of self-gratifying exploitation and abuse. In the book of Ezekiel, for example, we read a bitter indictment of the false shepherds of Israel who, instead of looking after the sheep, were taking advantage of those under their care (Ezek. 34.1–16). It is salutary to recognize that the phenomenon of pastoral abuse is nothing new.

Sadly for the churches, a large number of sexual scandals have recently brought issues of pastoral abuse under the spotlight of sustained, critical publicity. We explored in the last chapter some of the flashpoint areas where abuse of ministerial power leads to encroachment of sensitive boundaries, especially in the area of touch. But there is much more to spiritual and pastoral abuse than the flagrant sexual transgressions which lead to embarrassing headlines. Pastors need to be aware of the propensity for low level abuse which arises whenever the principles of good practice are misunderstood or deliberately set aside.

The notion of spiritual abuse has recently been defined as 'the mistreatment of a person in need of help, support or greater spiritual empowerment, with the result of weakening, undermining or decreasing that person's spiritual empowerment'.[10] It is important to recognize that any kind of poor practice can be actually abusive, and that religious mistreatment of vulnerable adults and children is not confined to individuals who are patently criminal or organizations which are readily recognized as cults.

A growing body of research reveals that abusive practices are not at all uncommon within mainstream churches. The fact that people are in ignorance of it does not make it any less of an issue. Indeed, because the very idea of spiritual abuse is something which church leaders find hard to countenance means that people who have experienced abusive individuals or communities at first hand can find it very difficult to share their pain and difficulties with any degree of acceptance or understanding.

The first step in combating this tragic state of affairs is to recall that power dynamics play a significant role in every pastoral relationship (see Chapter 9). This means that unless the inequalities of power are acknowledged, there is an unsurprising temptation for pastors to misuse the power of their position to satisfy their own needs at the expense of others. When this happens under the umbrella of a pastoral relationship which is supposed to be benign and caring, then the deep personal impact cuts to the heart of a person's faith, leaving a cruel legacy of bewilderment and spiritual betrayal.

In the pastoral context, common features of abusive relationships are as follows:

- The pastor cultivates an undue level of dependency.
- The pastor encourages exclusive relationships.
- The pastor behaves as if he or she always knows best.
- The pastor uses strongly loaded language to suggest divine authority for his or her advice and behaviour.
- The pastor discourages independent thinking and a questioning approach.
- The pastor's language inculcates a sense of shame, or fear, or anxiety.
- The pastor justifies intrusive visiting policies (e.g. in relation to vulnerable groups of elderly people or those in residential care settings).

---

10 David Johnson and Jeff VanVonderen, 1991, *The Subtle Power of Spiritual Abuse*, Minneapolis: Bethany House, p. 16.

- The pastor upholds strong patterns of discipline (e.g. heavy shepherding of adults and rigid nurture of young people).
- The pastor's ministry lacks wider accountability (or is accountable only within a small circle of like-minded ministers).
- The pastor fosters a culture which evades criticism and colludes with poor practice.

Do the abusers set out to inflict damage? In the majority of cases, they are unaware of the shadow side of their purportedly 'caring' agenda.

> They may, in fact, be convinced that their behaviour is what the Lord has mandated. What others interpret as control they may view as caring for the flock. They are usually so narcissistic or so focused on some great thing they are doing for God that they don't notice the wounds they are inflicting on their followers.[11]

Rarely has the shadow of abuse caused such damage to the reputation of the Christian gospel as in recent decades. Integrity of pastoral care must therefore be rooted in the maturity and wholeness of pastors who, knowing their own frailty and sinfulness, are unafraid to bring their motives and practices into the searching light of honest reflection and unshrinking accountability.

Guard your heart

> Above all else, guard your heart, for it is the wellspring of life. (Prov. 4.23, NIV)

First and last in the practice of Christian ministry, we find that the personal virtues of integrity and humility are the chief qualifications for authentic pastoral care. Gregory the Great's earnest advice remains as timely as ever.

> Necessity demands that one should carefully examine who it is that comes to the position of spiritual authority; and coming solemnly to this point, how he should rightly live; and living well, how he should teach; and teaching rightly,

---

11 Ronald Enroth, 1994, *Recovering from Churches that Abuse*, Grand Rapids: Eerdmans, p. 8.

with what kind of self-examination he should learn his own weakness. Necessity also demands that humility does not flee when the office is assumed.[12]

Pastoral care begins with the pastor. We recall from the first part of this book that the call to be human is an invitation to embrace fullness of life in Christ. Christ calls us to spiritual maturity for ourselves before we are commissioned to care for others. Generosity, authenticity, hospitality and compassion all grow from a deep personal knowledge of the gospel which is grounded in grace. For pastoral ministry to be sustained, therefore, we need to return constantly to the challenges of personal spiritual formation and integrity. The key elements of this ongoing ministerial formation can be summarized in terms of spirituality, structure, having someone to talk to, and self-awareness.

Spirituality

Healthy ministry is the fruit of calling, not drivenness. This means that the negative motivations arising from frustrated personal needs are displaced by the overflowing graciousness of God which constantly renews the wellsprings of pastoral compassion.

Frank Lake described the spiritual dynamics of ministry in terms of a 'cycle of grace', which overcomes the toxic drives of an unredeemed 'cycle of works'. This simple concept reflects that before any of us can bring care and compassion to others, we need first to receive a level of spiritual acceptance and emotional nourishment for ourselves. It is out of the deep springs of acceptance and well-being, which flow ultimately from the heart of God, that we discover our own resources of motivation and compassion to care.[13]

If this cycle is reversed, then a perverse set of dynamics works destructively not only within the soul of the pastor but also, tragically, within the very relationships in which she seeks to bring care. If the pastor's own life is insufficiently rooted in the love of God, then she will be driven by achievement rather than acceptance. Her need to find significance will drive an unwholesome pattern of

---

12 St Gregory the Great, 2007, *The Book of Pastoral Rule*, New Haven: St Vladimir's Seminary Press, p. 27.

13 Frank Lake, 1994, *The Dynamic Cycle: Introduction to the Model*, Oxford: Clinical Theology Association.

ministry which is geared towards the satisfaction of her own inner hunger rather than shaping a free and fulfilling self-offering for the sake of others. Frustration, anxiety, resentment, and even abuse are the sorry fruits of a pastoral ministry that struggles to sustain itself without the deep and ongoing nourishment of a spiritual life which is soaked in the love of God.

Structure

Sustaining a healthy spiritual life in ministry requires some kind of structure. Human beings are creatures of rhythm, created to find their well-being in harmony with the physical, biological and emotional rhythms of the natural world. Just as the cycle of grace works to sustain an inner spiritual 'flow' through the course of ministry, so a humble attention to the cycles of work and rest and prayer will be crucial in sustaining the outward commitments of pastoral ministry in humble service for others.

This fundamental insight was enshrined in the Christian tradition by the wise and humane practices of the *Rule of Saint Benedict* (see Chapter 7). Although the particular practices suited to a monastic life will not serve the interests of most contemporary pastors, the principle of structuring a rule of life is a good one to observe. In essence, this is about developing the kind of regular habits which will nurture the pastor's own well-being so that she is able to offer of her best to others. A typical rule of life will entail setting time aside from active ministry to live a rounded life, as well as factoring in time and energy to cultivate a deep relationship with God and sustaining friendships with loved ones.[14]

Someone to talk to

Integrity is not a solo pursuit. Even the most self-disciplined pastor knows that she also needs relationships of accountability and support to sustain her vocation and to encourage her ongoing development.

---

14 For guidance on adapting the *Rule of Saint Benedict* for today, see Esther de Waal, 1995, *A Life-Giving Way: A Commentary on the Rule of St Benedict*, London: Geoffrey Chapman; and Jane Tomaine, 2005, *St. Benedict's Toolbox: The Nuts and Bolts of Everyday Benedictine Living*, London: Morehouse Publishing.

We have already explored the value of some kind of pastoral supervision. But beyond the direct supervisory relationship, many pastors will be greatly enriched by wider networks of support and education – not least among their peers. It is not unusual, for example, for people who have trained together as pastoral workers or ordained ministers to create cell groups which meet together for ongoing prayer and confidential support in their ministries. The mutual understanding and fellowship which grew up over the course of their shared training is a precious resource to anchor them in the inevitable ups and downs of a demanding life of ministry.

Many pastors will also seek out specialist input from time to time. It is good to think in terms of some continuing study, perhaps in an area of personal expertise, which will stimulate lifelong learning in ministry. For some ministers, the rawness of their pastoral work will expose painful issues in their personal life; and it is a sign of healthy self-care in such cases for the pastor to seek out supportive counselling and advice.

Self-awareness

The pastor is called to be first and foremost a human being, fully alive, deeply self-aware and steadily growing in maturity in Christ. The essential mark of her integrity will be a fundamental honesty about who she is and how she relates to her role. With 'good enough' emotional intelligence, imagination and transparency, she can trust in the faithfulness of God's calling to renew the gifts that her ministry will demand.

For most of us, an element of good humour is one of the best ways to stay grounded in self-awareness. In that spirit, we might embrace the good advice laid out in the so-called 'Carer's Commandments'.

1. Thou shalt not try to be all things to all people.
2. Thou shalt not be perfect or even try.
3. Thou shalt leave undone things that ought to be done.
4. Thou shalt not spread thyself too thin.
5. Thou shalt learn to say no.
6. Thou shalt schedule time for thyself and thy supportive network.
7. Thou shalt switch off and do nothing regularly.

8   Thou shalt be boring, inelegant, untidy and unattractive at times.
9   Thou shalt not feel guilty.
10 Thou shalt not be thine own worst enemy.[15]

We have seen in this chapter that a capacity for pastoral care is never something to be taken for granted. Each pastor will need integrity and humility if she is to sustain her ministry against the acids of exhaustion, temptation and spiritual decay. The elements of good practice are not difficult to identify; but it will require determination and discipline to build and maintain the wise balance of accountability and support that will guard against abuse of self and others.

Above all else, for the sake of your pastoral calling, guard your heart.

Questions

Questions for private journaling or prayerful reflection

- Can you think of a critical incident which has prompted fresh questions about your pastoral role?
- Have you found someone to talk with about the issues raised by this incident?
- What new learning can you draw from the experience?

Questions for group discussion

- What does pastoral integrity mean for you?
- How can you develop a rule of life which will sustain you in your pastoral ministry?

Further Reading

Benyei, Candace R., 1998, *Understanding Clergy Misconduct in Religious Systems: Scapegoating, Family Secrets and the Abuse of Power*, Binghamton, NY: The Haworth Press.

---

15 Chris Edmondson, 2001, *Ministers Love Thyself: A Self Help Guide*, quoted in 'Holy Orders for a Stress-Free Life', *The Times* 26 January 2001.

Cameron, Helen, John Reader, Victoria Slater and Chris Rowland, 2012, *Theological Reflection for Human Flourishing*, London: SCM Press.

Campbell, Alastair V., 1986, *Rediscovering Pastoral Care*, 2nd edn, London: Darton, Longman and Todd.

Foskett, John and David Lyall, 1988, *Helping the Helpers: Supervision and Pastoral Care*, London: SPCK.

Green, Laurie, 2009, *Let's Do Theology: Resources for Contextual Theology*, London: Mowbray.

Hawkins, Peter and Robin Shohet, 2006, *Supervision in the Helping Professions*, Maidenhead: Open University Press.

Lamdin, Keith and David Tilley, 2007, *Supporting New Ministers in the Local Church*, London: SPCK.

Leach, Jane and Michael Paterson, 2010, *Pastoral Supervision*, London: SCM.

Lee, Carl and Sarah Horsman, 2002, *Affirmation and Accountability*, Dunsford: The Society of Mary and Martha.

Litchfield, Kate, 2006, *Tend My Flock: Sustaining Good Pastoral Care*, Norwich: Canterbury Press.

Nash, Sally and Paul Nash, 2009, *Tools for Reflective Ministry*, London: SPCK.

Ward, Frances, 2005, *Lifelong Learning*, London: SCM.

Whitehead, James D. and Evelyn Eaton Whitehead, 1995, *Method in Ministry: Theological Reflection and Christian Ministry*, Kansas City: Sheed and Ward.

Some helpful online resources are available from the Association of Pastoral Supervisors and Educators at http://www.pastoralsupervision.org.uk/

11

Messy Moments

Unsought, Untamed, Unimaginable Encounters

The cartoonist Dave Walker has a marvellous way of depicting the everyday quirks of church life. His cartoon on 'Leaving Church' shows a long queue of people all wanting to ask the vicar about something. 'Can I swap my reading?' 'Will you come and do a talk?' 'Would you like a barn dance ticket?' 'Will you visit my mother?' 'Will you baptize my children?' 'What time is Alpha?' 'Will you give me a reference?' 'Is that a new stole?' 'Are you going to Deanery Synod?' 'Can I arrange a confession?' 'Why don't we use the 1662?' 'Can I swap coffee rota slots?' 'Can we book the hall for a party?' 'Was that Eucharistic Prayer legal?' 'Can we sing some more modern songs?' 'Do we believe in purgatory?' 'Fancy a round of golf?' 'Shall we go to the pub?' 'Have I told you about my leg?'[1]

The sheer messiness of pastoral care is as bewildering as it is thrilling for most ministers, who encounter a vast range of people in and on behalf of the Church. One thing is certain: human encounters cannot be neatly contained in a series of tidy professional boxes. The reality of pastoral care is that it is a ministerial art that must be cultivated in and among the flow of life – in all its messiness and unpredictability. This chapter addresses the unique spontaneities that shape the kaleidoscope of pastoral care, exploring how each unsought, untamed, unimaginable encounter plays its part in the mysterious outworking of incarnational grace.

---

1 Dave Walker, *The Dave Walker Guide to the Church*, http://www.cartoonchurch.com [date accessed 1 September 2012].

In the thick of it

Authentic pastoral care happens in the midst of life. Somehow or other, quite often without the grace of forward planning, little breakthroughs come about because of an available pastoral presence that was committed to being human, being around and being good news. George Gammack described this typically pastoral mode of relating as a messy mixture of momentary meetings or, more briefly, a 'ministry of messy moments'.[2]

Most pastoral work cannot possibly be separated out from the rest of life. It is all mixed up within the general flow of human relationships. Caring and guiding, healing and challenging takes place all the time. It happens in impromptu moments at the back of church or on the corner of the street. It goes on among friends as well as strangers, regular worshippers as well as occasional callers. It strikes up on the back of the most ordinary email or the briefest of conversations. It takes place in all weathers, come rain or shine. It shows its face in the midst of happy days and horrible tragedies alike.

There is no way of avoiding the inherent messiness of this kaleidoscopic ministry. It is part and parcel of the incarnational business of walking alongside fellow human beings at their points of growth and discovery, struggle and pain. Of course, it places heavy demands on the pastor to hold herself open and attentive amid the swirling currents of everyday life and relationships. But it belongs to the adventurous nature of a uniquely Christian ministry of 'perilous paraklesis' to pick up the wind of the Spirit in whatever direction it may happen to blow.[3]

The pastoral moment

Travelling one day from Jerusalem in the south to Galilee in the north, Jesus and his disciples took the quickest route on foot through the region of Samaria. Tired and thirsty, Jesus sat down by the ancient well that traced its origins back to the patriarch Jacob. As Jesus' disciples set off towards the nearby town to buy

---

2 George Gammack, 2000, 'Ministry of Messy Moments', *Contact* 132, pp. 27–34.

3 The phrase 'perilous paraklesis' comes from Frank Lake, 1981, *Tight Corners in Pastoral Counselling*, London: Darton, Longman and Todd, pp. 74–5.

food, along the same road came a woman to draw water from the well. And so it was that her path crossed with that of Jesus the Messiah (John 4.1–30).

We read that a great deal of Jesus' ministry takes place 'along the way'. The Gospels portray him as always on the move: and yet, he is anything but unfocused. In the story of the woman at the well, as in so many other narratives, we notice how Jesus is poised, ready and alert to seize the moment. Despite the fact that in the territory of Samaria he has no formal authority or clear social standing, he negotiates a profoundly challenging conversation with a passing woman, which leads to radical transformation in her life.

To seize the moment and shape pastoral time is a matter of discerning the subtle intersections of *kairos* and *chronos*, when gracious opportunities for wisdom and transformation spring up in the midst of ordinary life. We saw in Chapter 3 how a sensitivity to the shifting spiritual challenges and developmental stages of life can alert pastors to *kairos* moments of particular openness to the renewing grace of God. Jesus understood this vital territory: he knew what was in every human heart (John 2.24–25). Perhaps in the depth of his humanity there was an intuitive recognition of the particular factors which led a Samaritan woman, on her own, to draw water at the height of the day. Certainly, in the ensuing conversation with Jesus, she encountered such wisdom and compassion that she invites her neighbours to 'Come and see a man who told me everything I have ever done!' (John 4.29).

Micro-transformations

Along the paths of everyday life the discerning pastor will become aware of countless gracious moments of opportunity, where a chance meeting or a brief encounter triggers something profound in another person's life. It may arise in the planned occasions of formal pastoral visiting in a home or institution. More commonly, the pastor learns to be attuned to those unsought, unexpected moments of micro-transformation, which spring up in the interstices of everyday life – after a meeting, over a coffee or at the school gates.

Being intentional about such ministry entails offering a habitual kind of presence which is open, available and expectant of transformation. Figure 11.1 depicts the pastoral dynamics of this ministry in terms of 'embracing' the moment. It is another way of depicting the pastoral encounter in terms of a threefold movement, this time centred on the dynamic of 'embrace'. I have drawn the motif of embrace from the Croatian theologian Miroslav Volf, who offers this as a dramatic image of transformative spiritual encounter.[4] Volf is not so much referring to a literal physical embrace (which is rarely appropriate in pastoral encounters) as to the dynamic relationship between the self and another which the embrace symbolizes and enacts.

Figure 11.1 Embracing the pastoral moment

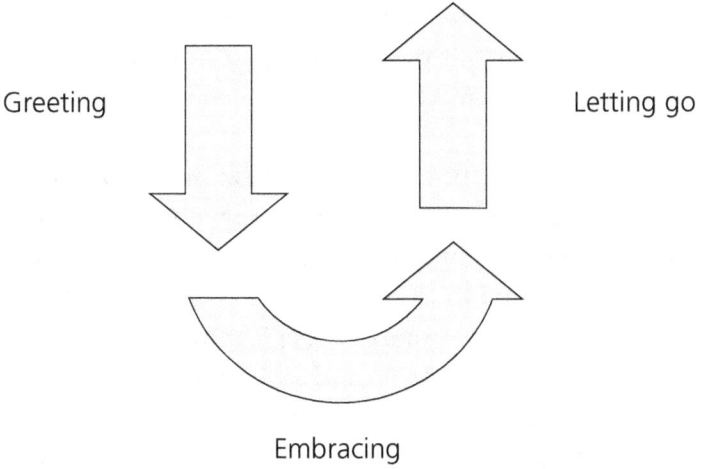

An embrace begins with a gesture of welcome. The one offering a greeting stands with open arms, making space emotionally and spiritually for another person to engage. Next follows a period of waiting. Will the offer be taken up? Or will the other person turn away? The pastor is always vulnerable to disinterest or disdain. But if he finds a reciprocating engagement, then some kind of openheartedness, some human tenderness can be exchanged. Two people become fully present, each to the other. A moment of intimacy, akin to the softness of embrace, allows them to share in an expression of deeper joys and struggles and cares. This moment must not be greedily prolonged, however. It is a time for understanding and communion, but not an occasion for possession and control. The embrace ends, therefore, as intentionally as it began, with the opening up and active release of letting go.

---

4 Miroslav Volf, 1996, *Exclusion and Embrace: A Theological Exploration of Identity, Otherness, and Reconciliation*, Nashville: Abingdon, pp. 140–5.

A similar dynamic patterns many of the more or less brief encounters of everyday pastoral ministry. The pastor's approach begins in welcoming acceptance of the other person. A smile, an outstretched hand, the opening rapport of a conversation attempts to gently invite the development of trust that will allow a deeper communication to develop. For Jesus, his exchange with the woman at the well began with simple banter about a free drink. In everyday life, the initial contact with a pastor might begin with the shared chit-chat about children's schooling, or the warm eye contact of the chaplain on the hospital corridor. The pastor who makes himself open in this way must inevitably risk embarrassment, dismissal or inconvenience. It is entirely possible that his gesture will be refused. But as he waits without pressure, he signals the kind of open-hearted welcome which accepts the other person on their own terms for the possibility of further engagement and conversation.

If the moment opens up, then the pastor enters into a new and deeper space of rich engagement. Like the tenderness of an embrace, this phase of deeper intimacy invites an exchange of joy and pain, struggle and blessing. Who knows what a work of transformation may be touched off by such encounters? The imagery of the embrace recalls, for example, one of the epic moments in the life of Jacob when he wrestles with an angel at the ford of Jabbok (Gen. 32.22–31). In one of the most suggestive narratives of the Old Testament, Jacob's night of wrestling with a mysterious stranger works out the undoing and transformation of a whole lifetime of tangled relationships with his brother. Jacob the wrestler emerges with renewed strength and spiritual integrity, blessed with a new name and noble identity, yet wounded forever through the loss of his old trickster ways of proud self-sufficiency.

There is nothing easy about engaging pastorally with other people's struggles. The pastor who comes close enough to enter into another person's tangled history must be prepared to hold on and to wrestle as the hard work of deep transformation yields to new and lasting spiritual growth.

At the end of the intense encounter, every authentic pastoral exchange concludes with a deliberate letting go. It is neither honest nor helpful to cling on to another person after the moment of pastoral intimacy has run its course. The transformation that has been wrought, however small or large, must be proved in the life that follows. It is not something to be grasped and controlled by a pastor who is greedy for recognition. This is the model we see in the ministry of Jesus where, typically, his miracles of healing conclude with a clear dismissal and return to the ongoing stream of life. (See, for example, Mark 5.19, Mark 8.26 and Luke 17.19.) Henri Nouwen emphasized the pastoral importance of leaving in relation to a ministry of visitation in the hospital or the home where 'it is essential for patients and parishioners to experience that it is good for them, not only that we come but also that we leave'. 'We have to learn to leave so that the Spirit may come.'[5]

Being alert to discern and embrace unexpected *kairos* moments is central to the incarnational business of Christian ministry. The artful shaping of these precious moments in the open field of everyday life is one of the most under-recognized skills of pastoral care. First, there is the warmth of beckoning acceptance, which opens up the possibility of transformation. Next, through deeply reciprocal presence and attention, the resources of growth and healing are powerfully engaged. And then in a final purposeful turn, when the encounter has drawn to its close, the hopeful pastor continues on his way – leaving room for the ongoing ministry of the Holy Spirit.

A lifetime burning in every moment

Something happens in the pastoral moment which is larger than a random intersection between two passing lives. This richer transformative experience was described by the astonished disciples who met the risen Jesus on the Emmaus road: 'Were not our hearts burning within us while he was talking to us on the road, while he was opening the scriptures to us?' (Luke 24.32). What took place in that memorable conversation served to reshape their understanding of all they had experienced in the past and to inform and inspire their hope for what might be possible in the future.

One of the fruits of effective pastoral care is a larger understanding of the shape of human experience. Sometimes this insight can be grasped in terms of abstract ideas, or theories or doctrines. More often, the transformative wisdom which enables fresh thinking and action comes to human beings in the form of stories. Our souls are stirred and our imagination is released by the power of a story, which makes sense of our experience in the past and points us forward to find new directions for the future. This seems to have been Ruth's experience

---

5 Henri Nouwen, 1977, *The Living Reminder*, New York: Seabury Press, p. 44.

Pastoral Story

Ruth started attending the evening service for healing after her mother's first stroke. She was not the kind of person to seek dramatic answers to prayer, but she had warmed to the description of a gentle service of Communion, where people who were ill themselves, or those carrying concerns for others, could gather together for mutual encouragement and prayer.

Being the only child of her elderly parents and a single woman with a career to maintain, Ruth felt the burden of invalid care very heavily. Her father had significant memory problems and was finding it hard to cope with organizing life at home. Now that her mother had been physically affected by a stroke, it had fallen to Ruth to visit daily to make sure that the basics of home life could continue.

When Ruth first arrived at the healing Eucharist, she was surprisingly moved by the atmosphere. There was a kindness and respect among all who attended which gave her the space to lay down some of her weariness and frustration. The sharing of Communion was infused with such tenderness that Ruth felt able to entrust the full weight of her burden to God's love. At the time for individual prayer and laying on of hands, she asked for patience for her mother and comfort for her father. The priest anointed Ruth's hands with oil for caring and prayed that she would know the sufficiency of Christ's strength day by day.

Ruth had not expected to attend the healing service more than once, but this monthly fellowship became a vital means of spiritual support throughout a difficult period. Each time she went to Communion, she found fresh resources to sustain her. The broken bread spoke of the frailty and the preciousness of life. The taste of wine, for all its bitter symbolism, brought a sweetness that spoke of new hope. The blessing that closed the service breathed a lasting peace into her soul.

in the service of healing. Through sharing in the bread and wine of the Eucharist, she found herself caught up in the healing narrative of Jesus' suffering, dying and rising to new life. As she received the anointing of sacred oil, she felt the personal reality of the Spirit's presence in deep consolation and enabling power.

Theologians in recent years have paid close attention to the power of narrative as a vehicle for Christian truth. It seems that the impact of a story operates at a deeper level of human understanding than the truths which are conveyed in simpler or more traditionally dogmatic modes. While it could be true and helpful to some extent to simply tell a person in Ruth's situation that God loves them and will strengthen them by his Spirit, Ruth found that it was the narrative experience of entering into the story of passion and resurrection, healing and anointing, which made a significant difference to her life.

What makes stories so powerful? Philosophers argue that the dynamic shape of a narrative works to bind together life events and human agents in a pattern that gives new meaning. A narrative brings purpose and direction to experiences which would otherwise be experienced as pointless or chaotic. So we do not tell stories merely to illustrate a point or to provide a colourful way of saying something which could be expressed more directly through propositional statements. We share stories as a way of creating meaning, because there is no other way that so richly shapes and re-evaluates the muddle of things that we experience in the course of messy human life in the world.

Stories, in other words, are an incarnational mode of truth-telling. For Christians, they make sense of what it means to be a child of God living in fellowship with Christ through the grace of the Spirit. They help us to recognize our own pilgrimage through life in all its seasons as part of a wider narrative of God's redemptive purpose for his creation.

Narratives of care

In any pastoral encounter, we can begin to understand the process of spiritual growth and transformation in terms of a telling and retelling of life's story. In this creative struggle, the role of the pastor is to envision and encourage by holding open a living connection with the great covenant story of faith.

Figure 11.2 Pastoral care as narrative interpretation

The story of the
Christian community   Pastoral   The particularity
and its tradition   ---- care ----   of life stories

Charles Gerkin portrays the pastor, in this respect, as a dialogical interpreter called to stand between the communal story of the Christian community and the many life stories of people who in some way relate to it.[6] The pastor must nurture the empathic skills of listening to and interpreting stories of human hurt and desperation, healing and hope. Then, picking up the deep resonances of particular life stories she lends her own voice to co-narrate a freshly meaningful expression of a human life in all its fullness and frailty.

In all this the pastor's contribution is more than an echoing voice. She too, as a member and representative of the Church, will be the bearer of an amazing story of immense spiritual power. The wonder of the incarnation, God drawing close to fragile humanity; the brokenness of the cross; the triumph of risen life; the endless possibility of new beginnings: these great themes resonate through her whole being, deeply shaping her vision of covenantal care and subtly reframing her narration of life events.

Like Jesus with the woman at the well, the pastor crafts into being a rich and creative, open and vulnerable, shared discovery of a story strong enough to live by. In the intimate dialogical encounter, this must always be a messy process because the story of good news will be constructed in the moment: a pre-packaged formula will scarcely touch the spot. And it will always be a vulnerable process because the pastor herself is implicated, involved and intimately committed to the truth she enacts and embodies: a disinterested prescription carries little power to heal.

---

6 Charles V. Gerkin, 1997, *An Introduction to Pastoral Care*, Nashville, Abingdon, pp. 111–12.

Picking up threads

The artfulness of the pastor lies in picking up those personal threads of life which can be stitched and woven into the larger narrative of the Christian story. To cultivate her art, the pastor needs to dwell deeply within the Christian story, to know its rhythm, to own its passion, to follow its direction. Living within the narrative of faith, she learns to recognize and reflect the play of its wisdom amid the currents and undertows of human encounters. Not that she should attempt to make a direct application of scriptural truth to every situation. The skill of the pastor is subtly different and much more dialogical than the proclamation of a preacher; but it is no less a vehicle of passionate good news.

By way of example, let us consider how a narrative reading of Luke's Gospel might shape the imagination of a pastor for the classic ministries of healing, sustaining, guiding and reconciling and the more radical ministries of resisting, empowering, nurturing and liberating (see Chapter 7).

- The story of the paralysed man (Luke 5.17–26) raises profound questions about the holistic nature of *healing* and the interplay between mind and body, person and relationships. It reflects the common experience of those who cannot plumb their own spiritual resources without help, needing the care and initiative of others to bring them to a point where healing might be possible. It's a story that comes alive whenever someone needs to rely on the kindness of friends and the prayers of strangers to get them through times when their own resources are at an end.
- Jesus' teaching on prayer (Luke 11.9–13) touches on the challenging issues of hope and expectancy. How do we understand the *sustaining* power of God when the experience of intercessory prayer may seem far from straightforward or satisfactory? On the face of it, we might think it a simple matter to ask, to seek, to knock. But the pastor has to reflect deeply and critically on what it means to trust a fatherly God whose good gifts are not always easy to recognize or to receive. These are sayings to savour when the struggle to believe in the goodness of God's love bites deep into the soul.
- The great parables of Jesus work artfully on human imagination to shape and mould attitudes and behaviour. The famous story of the Good Samaritan (Luke 10.29–37) has become one of the *guiding* narratives of Western culture, pointing up the personal impact of a compassionate presence, and

motivating carers to focus on the small things they can do for others. This is a story to walk through in prayerful imagination time and again, if we are not to grow weary in doing good (cf. Gal. 6.9).
- Jesus' graphic teaching about forgiveness (Luke 6.37–42) puts our natural human judgementalism into sharper perspective. The work of *reconciling* people with themselves, with one another and with God begins with clear-sightedness. Putting aside the blinkers – or removing the proverbial log – from our eyes is the first step towards a more generous experience of fullness of living. This is essential teaching for anyone in a position of authority over the lives of others.
- Jesus' determination to heal on the sabbath (Luke 6.6–11) promotes outrage but demonstrates the importance of confrontation with evil structures. *Resisting* unjust or abusive behaviours and attitudes and contesting the false priorities that undermine the full dignity of people's lives are crucial, if sometimes unpopular, expressions of compassion. Stories of liberation are a powerful resource for those called to galvanize opinion and work for a more just and inclusive society.
- Mary's wonderful Magnificat (Luke 2.46–55) celebrates the good news of *empowering* that comes to birth in Christ. Her fervent advocacy and tenderness on behalf of all the powerless of the world reflects God's commitment to raising up those who have previously been stripped of authority and power. Women in particular need stories and role models which raise up their God-given vocation in Christ.
- There is a similar radical edge to Jesus' teaching on new wine and new wineskins (Luke 5.36–39). Thoughtful pastors recognize that there is much more to *nurturing* than kindness and sympathy. Real spiritual growth requires a vigorous commitment to the love that makes space for difficult change and development. Stories of subversion are important tools against complacency and heedless conservatism in the Church.
- Jesus' encounters with those who were written off by polite society reflect the importance of reaching into the forgotten corners of the world so that the *liberating* power of God might be unleashed. His respect for the sinful woman in the house of a Pharisee (Luke 7.36–50) shows a profound concern for those unjustly afflicted and an astonishing commitment to releasing them into fullness of life as people created, redeemed and loved by God.

Linking these stories to the wider purposes of pastoral care illustrates something of the interpretive role of the mature pastor. The humble image of picking up threads is well suited to the tentativeness of most everyday pastoral encounters. We are not proposing that some great work of salvation will be evident in each chance pastoral meeting. What matters is that the faithful pastor learns to attend to human stories with same the creative confidence, which she has learned from the gospel.

Her task then will be to pick up threads of human experience which can be patiently woven into an unfolding tapestry of kingdom beauty. It would be arrogant to presume that the pastor can even begin to see the full picture. Her calling is to attend to each momentary intersection of *kairos* and *chronos*. In this moment, where the details of human life can be opened up and drawn forward, like the warp and woof of the weaver's loom, she hopes to weave small threads within the wider frame of God's covenantal purpose for all creation.

> **Take this moment**
>
> Take this moment, sign and space;
> Take my friends around;
> Here among us make the place
> Where your love is found.
>
> John Bell[7]

The pastor's own life is a tapestry of moments in which she seeks to be available to others through being available to God.

The skills we have alluded to in this chapter are not easy to define. They depend on a quality of prayerful relationship which is a wellspring of discernment and compassion in the messy *kairos* moments of ordinary life.

This quality of prayerful attentiveness cannot be turned on at a moment's notice. It must be cultivated slowly and tenderly, like a bud that is ready to bloom when the time is right. The power in any pastoral moment comes from the Holy Spirit, whose venturesome love impels us to be alongside others at

---

7 John Bell, 1989, 'Take This Moment', from *Love from Below*, Glasgow: Wild Goose Publications, p. 86.

key times. Often we will have no clear sense or know how or why this gracious opportunism comes about. It is the intuitive sensation, the prayerful hunch, the inner voice of the heart which prompts the pastor to embrace this or that passing moment.

How does the Holy Spirit direct these encounters? There is no magical formula for pastoral discernment. There is simply the ongoing life of prayerful availability to God which flows, like a deep underground watercourse, through the soul of the pastor. Some of this is laid down in the regular disciplines of prayer, through a steadfast, loving, open-hearted ministry of intercession for others over months and years and a deep and loving familiarity with the truthful stories of the Christian gospel. It is all this prayerful wisdom and compassion which is gathered up in the moment, in a faithful entrusting to Christ of each encounter which is embraced in his name.

Moments of calm

Pastors who trade in messy moments will gather up a great deal of life's joys and sorrows along the way. If they are learning from Jesus, they will wisely step back from their ministry from time to time to rest awhile and regain the perspective which is essential for their spiritual poise. Building in sensible rhythms of personal space and sabbath time is an essential kind of spiritual hygiene, which clears away the accumulated chaos of other people's messiness, so that God can continue his work of patient weaving in the stories of our own lives.

Most important of all for the pastor are the moments of reflection that return her to the loving source of her vocation.

> 'What can I do?'
> Respect that question.
> Trust that you, one man, one woman,
> can do for God what otherwise would not be done.
> Trust that some people will hear the gospel of Jesus,
> that some who are in need will find the touch of human love,
> that others will find a listening ear or a voice in their poverty,

> only because you have chosen to give to God
> a central place in your life …
> It is not just your work, your choice, your decision.
> You choose because you are chosen,
> you choose because in the heart of your desire to love,
> you have found the heart of God searching for you.[8]

Questions

Questions for private journaling and theological reflection

- Think of a recent moment which opened up into a significant pastoral opportunity.
- Reflect on your approach to the encounter in each phase of greeting, embracing and letting go.
- What were the points which seemed to be most fruitful, or least fruitful, in the encounter?
- What new learning can you draw from reflecting on this moment?

Questions for group discussion

- Which of the narratives from Luke's Gospel shed fresh light on your pastoral encounters?
- How does your understanding of gospel stories explicitly or implicitly shape your response to the human stories you hear in pastoral encounters?
- What other Christian narratives are of particular importance in your pastoral ministry?

Further Reading

Bidwell, Duane R., 2004, *Short-Term Spiritual Guidance,* Minneapolis: Augsburg Fortress Press.

---

8 *Come Follow Me* (Pastoral of the Irish Bishops), 1989. From Donal Neary, 1994, *Forty Masses with Young People*, Dublin: The Columba Press, pp. 122–3.

Capps, Donald, 2001, *Giving Counsel: A Minister's Guidebook*, St Louis, Missouri: Chalice Press.
Gammack, George, 2000, 'Ministry of Messy Moments', *Contact*, 132, pp. 27–34.
Gerkin, Charles V., 1997, *An Introduction to Pastoral Care*, Nashville: Abingdon.
Lyall, David, 2001, *Integrity of Pastoral Care*, London: SPCK.
Peterson, Eugene H., 1993, *The Contemplative Pastor: Returning to the Art of Spiritual Direction*, Grand Rapids: Eerdmans.
Scott, David, 1997, *Moments of Prayer*, London: SPCK.

12

The Paradoxical Pastor

For us, there is only the trying. The rest is not our business. (T. S. Eliot)[1]

In a refreshingly candid exposition of the art of teaching, one of the more thoughtful commentators writes of 'the value of not always knowing what one is doing'.[2] This author faces a similar sense of bemusement at the end of a study guide which has been attempting to teach what pastors ought to be doing – or ought, at least, to be thinking about what they are doing. For in Christian ministry the humble practitioner is keenly aware of innumerable situations in which the deepest value must rest precisely in *not* knowing what one is doing!

'You'll never know how much that conversation helped me.' Time and again the significance of pastoral care is proved in ways that transcend any rational explanation. The pastor simply does not know, and often cannot know, whether or why or how her ministry will have any lasting effectiveness. The greater part of her work remains mysterious, hidden in Christ. This is not to say, of course, that ignorance and careless amateurism should be worn as a badge of pastoral pride. But it is to offer a serious caution against the wrong kind of confidence in our ministerial learning and hard-won professionalism.

Strange to say at the end of a carefully constructed study guide, but the teaching of pastoral theology as a rational discipline in books and classrooms can only take us so far. The sacred study of what it means to be human and what it takes to care is something which demands a whole lifetime of loving enquiry. In the open field of Christian discipleship, the humble pastor stumbles on deep mysteries in every aspect of her vocation, finding that both the call to be human and the call to care are shot through with immense and irresolvable paradox.

---

1 T. S. Eliot, 1969, 'East Coker', in *The Complete Poems and Plays*, London: Faber & Faber, p. 182.
2 Terry Atkinson and Guy Claxton, (eds), 2000, *The Intuitive Practitioner: On the value of not always knowing what one is doing*, Maidenhead: Open University Press.

Clay pots and transcendent treasure

> Not that we are competent of ourselves to claim anything as coming from us; our competence is from God. (2 Cor. 3.5)

> We have this treasure in clay jars, so that it may be made clear that this extraordinary power belongs to God and does not come from us. (2 Cor. 4.7)

The apostle Paul's experience of ministry was one of profound paradox. Strength and weakness, wisdom and folly, suffering and joy, life and death, bore in on his soul with inescapable ambiguity as he grappled with the mystery of living out the call of the gospel. It is this mystery that marks the authentic pastor. All the seeming contradictions of gospel-shaped living must be deeply embraced if we are to be true to our God-inspired calling.

There is always, though, the temptation to play safe, to hide behind the armour of expertise and professionalism, which puts us on a different footing from other human beings. But the world is not divided into gracious givers and the needy recipients of their care. Being truly human means embracing the essential vulnerability of our own condition as the indispensible prerequisite for walking alongside our brothers and sisters in Christ.

Henri Nouwen memorably captured this paradoxical aspect of Christian ministry in his reflections on the role of the wounded healer.[3] This archetypal image draws from ancient Greeks myths of the physician with an incurable wound, reflecting the biblical figure of the stricken Messiah, who is lifted up as a sign of healing and eternal life (Isa. 53.4–5; cf. John 3.14–15). The same metaphor was used by Carl Jung in a deeply sensitive study of the paradoxical character of the emotional healing which is only possible because of the woundedness of the so-called 'healer'. The therapist will be ineffective if he tries to function from a higher position of detachment. He must embrace the relationship between equals, because 'only the wounded physician heals'.[4]

This vision of ministry calls us far beyond the clear-cut benchmarks of competence, or professionalism, or technocratic effectiveness, to the transcendent space of mutual vulnerability to the risks and responsibilities of life in God's

---

3 Henri Nouwen, 1972, *The Wounded Healer*, New York, Doubleday.
4 Carl Jung, 1963, *Memories, Dreams, Reflections*, transl. R. & C. Winston, New York: Pantheon Books, p. 134.

world. We are called as pastors, not to hide or escape from our own brokenness and humanity, but to enter more deeply into the mysteries of human frailty, where we must mine the treasures of spiritual beauty which God gives to those who trust in his steadfast love.

Paradoxically, this means that pastors must grow stronger through perplexity, through tumults and difficulties, through personal anguish and sometimes through being blown off course. Some things cannot be discovered until we ourselves have been touched by the fires of affliction and have drunk from deep wells of consoling grace (cf. 2 Cor. 1.3–7). Only in yielding to the helplessness of undefended human woundedness and struggle can we know with assurance the embrace of sublime, transcendent, unconquerable love.

Much of this struggle will be fleshed out in encounters with those whom we attempt to care for. The overwhelming goodness of God will come alive where we are most humbly and transparently present to the humanity of our brothers and sisters, and so to ourselves.

> This is the mystery of the Christian ministry. When you open your house for the stranger, you might become the guest. When you minister, you are ministered to by those you have invited. When you speak about God to your friends, you find Him in your midst ... The paradox of the ministry indeed is that we will find the God we want to give in the lives of the people to whom we want to give him.[5]

For us pastors, then, there remains only the trying. There is only the responding, day by day, to the inviting call to be human and the insistent call to care. In trying and in responding, we expand our hope in such a way that we can take on board all the ambiguity and disappointment of life. We enliven our faith so that with risk and abandon we can follow Christ along the way that leads through the cross to glorious new life. We enlarge our love to enter deeply into the afflictions of others with all the tenderness and compassion of Christ.[6]

The rest is not our business.

---

5 Henri Nouwen, 2003, *Creative Ministry*, New York: Doubleday, p. 63.
6 Phil Zylla, 2007–8, 'What Language Can I Borrow? Theopoetic Renewal in Pastoral Theology', *McMaster Journal of Theology and Ministry* 9, p. 137.

Questions

Questions for private journaling and theological reflection

- Read the description of the servant of God in Isaiah 53. How do you understand the paradoxical power of the wounded healer in the life of Christ?
- How have you experienced something of this paradoxical ministry in your own life?

Further Reading

Campbell, Alastair V., 1986, *Rediscovering Pastoral Care*, London: Darton, Longman and Todd.

Dykstra, Robert C., 2005, *Images of Pastoral Care: Classic Readings*, St Louis, MS: Chalice Press.

Nouwen, Henri J. M., 2003, *Creative Ministry*, New York: Doubleday.

Veling, Terry A., 2005, *Practical Theology: "On Earth as it is in Heaven"*, New York: Maryknoll.

Sources and Acknowledgements

Wendell Berry: 'No, no, there is no going back' from *Collected Poems*, copyright © 1998, by permission of Counterpoint Press.

Kathy Galloway: 'Over Coffee' from *Love Burning Deep*, copyright © 1993, by permission of SPCK Publishers.

Janet Morley: 'At a Funeral' and 'Te Deum' from *All Desires Known*, copyright © 1988, by permission of SPCK Publishers.

Edwin Muir: 'The Annunciation' from *Collected Poems*, copyright © 1963, by permission of Faber and Faber Limited.

Donal Neary SJ: 'What can I do?' from *Forty Masses for Young People*, copyright © 1994, by permission of the Columba Press.

David Scott: 'Parish Visit' from *Selected Poems*, copyright © 1998, by permission of the Bloodaxe Books.

Index of Scriptural Passages

Genesis 1.31	22
Genesis 2.7	22
Genesis 9.8–17	4
Genesis 12—15	4
Genesis 12.1	22
Genesis 32.22-31	180
Genesis 37—50	32
Exodus 19—24	4
Deuteronomy 6.5	124
Deuteronomy 29—30	4
Job 28.12	30
Psalm 8	17–18
Psalm 13.1–2, 5–6	71
Psalm 23.4	85
Psalm 27.8–9	74
Psalm 31.3	74
Psalm 34.1	22
Psalm 38.21–22	74
Psalm 56.3	74
Psalm 66.10	38
Psalm 71	33
Psalm 78.72	158
Psalm 90	21
Psalm 95.7	22
Psalm 103.13–14	23
Psalm 103.13–17	69
Psalm 103.15	21
Psalm 104.27–30	69
Psalm 131.2	61
Psalm 136	4,22
Psalm 145.4	38
Psalm 145.9	20
Proverbs 4.23	170
Proverbs 17.3	38
Proverbs 25.11	136
Ecclesiastes 3.11	21
Song of Solomon	57,67
Isaiah 49.14–16	71
Isaiah 51.3	23
Isaiah 53	194
Isaiah 53.4–5	192
Isaiah 66.10–11	4
Ezekiel 34.1–16	168
Ezekiel 34.7-16	9
Matthew 7.24–27	40
Matthew 8.2	152
Matthew 8.23–27	94
Matthew 10.16	157
Matthew 11.4	27
Matthew 16.19	114
Matthew 18.1–3	45
Matthew 25.31–46	111

INDEX OF SCRIPTURAL PASSAGES

Matthew 26.38	61	Acts 20.28	123, 163
Matthew 28.20	135		
		Romans 6.3–4	38
Mark 1.11	22	Romans 8.11	23
Mark 1.35–38	154	Romans 8.38–39	72
Mark 5.19	181	Romans 12.2	40
Mark 8.26	181	Romans 12.4–8	109
Mark 8.36	111	Romans 15.7	118
Luke 2.46–55	186	1 Corinthians 3.3	55
Luke 2.52	22, 28	1 Corinthians 10.16	112
Luke 5.17–26	185	1 Corinthians 12.27	24
Luke 5.36–39	186	1 Corinthians 13.12	13
Luke 6.6–11	186	1 Corinthians 15.22	22
Luke 6.36	134		
Luke 6.37–42	186	2 Corinthians 1.3–4	72
Luke 7.36–50	186	2 Corinthians 1.3–7	193
Luke 8.5–8	138	2 Corinthians 2.16	82
Luke 8.45	152	2 Corinthians 3.5	192
Luke 10.29–37	185	2 Corinthians 3.18	33
Luke 11.9–13	185	2 Corinthians 4.7	76, 192
Luke 12.12	137	2 Corinthians 10.15	40
Luke 15.3–7	111		
Luke 17.19	181	Galatians 3.2–3	55
Luke 23.46	61	Galatians 4.4	22
Luke 24.32	181	Galatians 4.19	40
Luke 24.49	135	Galatians 5.16–21	55
		Galatians 6.2	8
John 1.14	20	Galatians 6.9	186
John 1.47	158	Galatians 6.10	112
John 2.24-25	178		
John 3.6–7	38	Ephesians 4.14	30
John 3.14–15	192	Ephesians 4.15–16	95
John 4.1–30	178	Ephesians 4.15	33, 40
John 6.67–68	44	Ephesians 4.16	88
John 9.2–3	25	Ephesians 5.25–32	57
John 10.1–16	9		
John 10.10	19, 30	Philippians 1.9	40
John 14.1	135	Philippians 2.1–4	112
John 14.18	135	Philippians 2.1–8	107
John 14.26	135	Philippians 2.12–13	40
John 14.27	135	Philippians 3.3–4	55
John 15.2	38		
John 17.19	13	Colossians 1.10	40
John 17.22–23	25	Colossians 2.9	54
		Colossians 2.19	88, 95
Acts 2.44–45	112	Colossian 3.3–4	40
Acts 4.32–37	112	Colossians 3.10	55
Acts 10.38	107	Colossians 3.12–17	4

Colossians 4.6	137	James 1.19	128
		James 3.1–11	151
1 Thessalonians 3.12	40		
1 Thessalonians 4.1	40	1 Peter 1.7	38
		1 Peter 2.2	40
2 Thessalonians 1.3	40	1 Peter 5.1–4	111
1 Timothy 3.2	163	2 Peter 1.3–4	112
		2 Peter 1.5–8	33
Hebrews 8.6	4	2 Peter 3.18	40
Hebrews 12.1–2	40		
		1 John 1.2–4	112
James 1.19–26	151	1 John 4.19	3

General Index

abuse 64, 118, 151–152, 168–172
accountability 112, 115, 122, 162–174
adolescence 6, 35–37, 42, 50, 61
adulthood 35–37, 44, 62
Aelred of Rievaulx 10
Ainsworth, Mary 73
anointing 81, 152, 182–183
anthropology
   cultural anthropology 29, 96
   theological anthropology 23–31, 71, 116
anxiety 6, 73, 75, 94–95, 116, 158, 164, 169
attachment 34–36, 61, 72–86, 88–97
attention 11, 77, 113, 116, 128, 130, 151, 181
Augustine, Saint 31, 33, 51, 54–55, 114
authority 18, 29, 42–43, 65, 94, 114, 145–146, 167, 169, 186
availability 12, 128, 130, 132, 135, 153–154, 177, 187–188

baptism 38, 42, 97, 99
Baxter, Richard 116
Benedict, Saint 112, 172
bereavement 47, 68–86, 90
body 23–24, 54–55, 58, 59, 147
Body of Christ 4, 24, 30, 38, 88, 92, 109, 122, 138, 162
boundaries 12, 13, 114, 141–155, 162, 163, 168
Bowlby, John 36, 73, 86
Bridges, William 39
Buber, Martin 127

calling 11, 17, 18, 20, 88, 105, 171, 173, 187, 192
care 1, 3–9, 32, 37, 68, 70, 71, 76, 78, 80, 83, 100, 105–124, 128–129, 143, 157, 163, 171, 183

chaplaincy 35, 78, 99, 110, 122, 137, 180
childhood 6, 19, 36, 41–42, 49, 61, 69, 73
children 19, 24, 41–42, 49, 73, 99, 121, 148, 151, 156, 169
chronos 21, 178, 187
Church 2, 4, 9, 12, 30, 45, 66, 68, 72, 84, 87–101, 111–120, 122, 123, 145, 162
Climacus, John 33
communication 66, 93, 126–139, 167, 168, 180
community 2, 4, 8, 12, 24, 26, 37, 38, 42, 43, 44, 45, 62, 65, 77, 78, 83, 87–101, 105, 110, 111–121, 128, 154, 184
compassion 1– 5, 7, 8, 11, 12, 20, 21, 68, 69, 71, 78, 84, 85, 110, 128, 132, 134, 152, 167, 171, 178, 185, 186, 187, 188, 193
confession 81, 85, 114, 150
confidentiality 150–151, 163–164, 173
conflict 36, 93, 97, 144, 161, 168
congregations 25, 89, 92
congruence 131, 133, 135
conversation 8, 121, 126–140, 149–150, 166, 177, 178, 180, 181, 191
conversion 38, 40, 46, 47, 54
counselling 8, 29, 77, 78, 79, 81, 82, 85, 116, 117, 122, 128, 132, 133, 163, 173
covenant 3–5, 6, 11, 12, 20, 47, 63, 70–72, 78, 80, 94, 95, 105, 107, 127, 157, 183, 184, 187
creation 4, 17, 20, 23, 45, 55, 58, 107, 166, 183, 187
crisis 35, 38, 41, 42, 47, 72, 74–78, 85, 96, 139, 146
critical incident analysis 166
cross 38, 55, 59, 72, 184, 193
cura animarum 113–114

death 21, 22, 38, 39, 40, 63, 68–72, 79–85, 98, 154, 192
dependence 7, 8, 9, 36, 42, 61, 69, 70, 73, 142, 169
desire 51–67, 162, 189
development 25, 26, 28, 32–48, 51, 52, 60–64, 73, 127, 178, 186
disability 19, 23, 24, 25, 75, 122, 152
discipline 57, 66, 112, 113, 114–115, 133, 150, 153, 166, 174, 188
doctrine 11, 24, 26, 55, 58, 84, 107, 116, 181
dualism 23, 54–56, 147
dual relationships 146

education 11, 57, 60–64, 112, 116, 136, 164, 165, 173
emails 76, 126, 135, 139, 144, 177
emotions 7, 41, 42, 43, 47, 60, 61, 72, 73–75, 77, 79, 83, 90–94, 96, 128, 131–134, 142, 147, 152, 153, 160, 161, 164, 165, 171–173, 179, 192
empathy 7, 77, 83, 133, 134, 136, 137, 184
Erikson, Erik 35, 37–38, 41, 49, 73
eschatology 27, 112
ethics 79, 147, 150, 151
Eucharist 21, 40, 66, 80, 97, 100, 112, 152, 182–183
evangelism 13

faith development 40–48
family 6–7, 19, 20, 23, 24, 25, 38, 43, 62, 76, 91, 94, 95, 98, 145, 153, 161
feminism 8, 117, 123
flourishing 19–30, 51, 87, 94, 154
forgiveness 5, 24, 79, 92, 97, 186
Fowler, James 40–49
Freud, Sigmund 31, 34, 61
friendship 6–7, 19, 24–25, 35, 76, 82, 84, 89, 90, 144, 146–147, 149, 153, 155, 162, 172, 177, 185, 193
funerals 6, 70, 76–77, 84, 98

Galloway, Kathy 127
gender 146, 152, 165
grace 3, 5, 12, 17, 20, 21, 24, 25, 26, 27, 33, 37, 40, 44, 47, 52, 57, 61, 63, 64, 82, 85, 88, 92, 95, 97, 100, 101, 106, 111, 118, 128, 132, 135, 137, 139, 162, 171, 172, 176, 177, 178, 183, 193
Gregory the Great 113, 115, 124, 170
grief 6, 23, 47, 68–86, 92, 132

group behaviour 87–101
guidelines 148, 154, 155, 156

healing 1, 4, 5, 17, 23, 24, 37, 44, 68, 70, 78–79, 80, 81, 83, 84, 92, 93, 94, 95, 96, 97, 101, 120, 122, 132, 134, 136, 142, 151, 177, 180, 181, 182–183, 184, 185, 186, 192
helping personality 162, 164
history of pastoral care 79, 91, 105, 111–124, 152, 168
holiness 52, 54, 66, 154
Holy Spirit 20, 33, 40, 55, 57, 65, 88, 97, 100, 120, 123, 135, 137, 181, 187, 188
homosexuality 62–63
hope 1, 4, 5, 6, 26–27, 32, 33, 36, 38, 40, 51, 55, 63, 66, 68, 71, 79, 80, 82, 84, 94, 96, 112, 120, 128, 129, 132, 135, 154, 181, 182, 184, 185, 193
hospital 78, 99, 108, 110, 122, 126, 180, 181
hospitality 24, 78, 99, 118–120, 128, 129, 130, 159, 171
humility 1–14, 21, 23, 27, 28, 29, 44, 45, 62, 76, 78, 82, 100, 101, 106, 107, 122, 123, 126, 137, 138, 139, 145, 170, 171, 172, 174, 191

Ignatius Loyola, Saint 57, 116
imagination 3, 4, 7, 8–10, 34, 41–42, 55, 66, 97, 99, 111, 128, 134, 137, 173, 181, 185
incarnation 3, 11, 12, 20, 55, 58, 59, 106, 107, 134, 135, 137, 139, 143, 176, 177, 181, 183, 184,
infancy 34, 35, 36, 41, 61, 73, 127
integrity 2, 3, 10, 13, 24, 37, 63, 78, 96, 118, 123, 128, 133, 141, 142, 144, 145, 148, 151, 155, 157–174, 180
intentionality 77, 81, 106–107, 126, 129, 130, 132, 135, 144, 164, 166, 178, 179
intercession 106, 188

kairos 5, 21, 37, 81, 178, 181, 187
koinōnia 106, 112–113

Lake, Frank 171, 177
language 28, 38, 41, 57, 66, 67, 74, 83, 97, 99, 119, 136–138, 151, 169
lay ministry 2, 97, 99, 109, 112, 117, 122, 141, 145, 149, 153, 165
leadership 13, 44, 46, 67, 89, 113, 114, 118, 121, 145, 147
liberation 4, 55, 59, 117–118, 124, 185, 186

life cycle 35–38, 48, 49–50, 60, 61, 93, 98
listening 13, 77, 81, 83, 126–140, 184, 188
liturgy 70, 81, 95–100, 121, 136
loss 6, 23, 63, 68–86, 92, 93
love 1, 3–5, 12, 13, 17–30, 33, 36, 40, 51– 67, 71, 72, 76, 78, 79, 80, 82, 84, 88, 92, 94, 95, 97, 100, 101, 105, 106, 111, 112, 119, 120, 122, 124, 128, 132, 135, 148, 149, 154, 159, 162, 171, 172, 182, 186, 187, 188, 193

management 163, 164, 167
marriage 43, 57, 62, 98, 100
maturity 5, 6, 11, 24, 25, 30, 32–48, 52, 59, 60–64, 66, 74, 87, 88, 95, 96, 99, 100, 101, 127, 129, 132, 138, 143, 147, 155, 158, 159, 162, 170, 171, 173, 187
mediation 168
meetings 121, 126, 153, 178, 187
mental health 6, 19, 85, 109, 120, 122, 142
midlife 35, 37, 43–44, 50
mission 13, 30, 123, 154
monasticism 57, 78, 112, 172
money 7, 64, 74, 112, 117
music 65, 96, 97
mutuality 5, 8, 24–26, 62, 63, 64, 79, 88, 100, 112, 115, 119, 121, 127, 128, 136, 147, 165, 168, 173, 182, 192

narrative 4, 6, 20, 22, 23, 26, 27, 33, 42, 132, 135, 178, 180, 183–184, 185, 186
non-verbal communication 96, 130, 131
Nouwen, Henri 86, 119, 134, 181, 192, 193, 194

old age 33, 37–38, 40, 50, 63, 109, 122, 146, 169

parables 111, 137, 185
paradox 9, 13, 21, 27, 44, 154, 191–194
pastoral theology 1–13, 21, 64, 100, 105, 113, 123, 141, 191
postmodernism 70, 86
power 8, 20, 23, 24, 25, 29, 44, 52, 56, 57, 61, 65, 78, 84, 88, 91, 93, 96, 97, 100, 111, 118, 124, 128, 132, 134, 135, 141, 145–146, 149, 152, 155, 160, 163, 167, 168, 169, 183, 184, 185, 186, 187, 192, 194
prayer 1, 3, 7, 10, 26, 65, 67, 68, 70, 71, 76, 78, 81, 82, 84, 89, 91, 99, 101, 106, 110, 112, 121, 122, 134, 149, 153, 154, 167, 172, 173, 182, 185, 186, 187, 188

preaching 13, 97, 112, 121, 136, 149, 185
presence 12, 68, 74, 75, 76, 78, 80, 81, 89, 91, 92, 95, 106, 107, 110, 114, 120, 128, 129, 132, 133, 135, 143, 145, 159, 160, 177, 178, 181, 183, 185
priests 81, 85, 97, 100, 106, 113, 114, 115, 135, 150, 182
professionalism 1, 5, 8, 12, 13, 14, 76, 78, 85, 95, 107, 110, 116, 120, 147, 148, 153, 155, 191, 192
projection 9, 65, 95, 161
psychology 2, 5, 7, 25, 28, 29, 33, 34, 38, 39, 60, 61, 70, 72, 73, 83, 90, 91, 94, 96, 97, 100, 115, 116, 117, 142, 164, 166
psychotherapy 29, 78, 116, 120, 122
Putnam, Robert 92

questions 3, 11, 13, 18, 38, 43, 61, 71, 72, 120, 130–131, 137, 166, 169, 188

reconciliation 79, 81, 97, 101, 114, 123, 185, 186
redemption 20, 23, 30, 38, 51, 54, 58, 59, 63, 64, 65, 66, 97, 105, 166, 183, 186
reflective practice 2, 6, 66, 110, 128, 134, 147, 165–167, 170, 188
relationships 2, 4, 5, 8, 12, 20, 21, 22, 24–26, 34, 35, 36, 37, 38, 40, 41, 42, 43, 47, 57, 59, 60, 61, 62, 64, 71, 73, 74, 80, 87–101, 105, 106, 107, 110, 114, 116, 121, 126, 127, 132, 133, 134, 138, 141, 142, 143, 144, 145, 146, 147, 148, 150, 152, 155, 159, 160, 162, 163, 164, 165, 166, 167, 168, 169, 171, 172, 173, 177, 180, 185, 192
repentance 37, 38, 114, 150
respect 7, 13, 28, 51, 90, 92, 93, 100, 109, 100, 129, 133, 139, 141, 142, 145, 149, 153, 165, 167, 182, 186
responsibility 29, 37, 43, 89, 109, 116, 121, 123, 143, 144, 147, 148, 149, 151, 153, 162, 167, 192
rest 27, 51, 112, 153, 172, 188
resurrection 4, 20, 22, 38, 40, 55, 72, 181, 183, 184
Ricoeur, Paul 44
rites of passage 98–99
rituals 29, 42, 87, 93, 95–101, 152
Rogers, Carl 133
role-awareness 2, 9, 29, 80–82, 94, 95, 106, 113, 120, 121, 123, 145, 146, 147, 153, 157–163, 173, 183
rule of life 172, 174

sacraments 22, 38, 40, 42, 66, 78, 79, 80, 85, 88, 96, 97, 99, 112, 114, 128, 150
safeguarding 64, 141, 147–148, 155–156
Saunders, Cicely 79
science 2, 25, 28–30, 38, 60, 75, 83, 115, 134
Scott, David 107–109
scripture 3, 4, 9, 17, 20, 21, 22, 32, 42, 54, 55, 57, 69, 71, 72, 111, 116, 124, 158, 166, 181
self-awareness 9, 36, 43, 65, 76, 78, 123, 126, 133, 134, 144, 145, 149, 153, 158, 160–162, 170, 171, 173–174, 191
Senge, Peter 39
sexuality 25, 34, 51–67, 118, 143, 147–148, 152, 162, 168
shepherd 9, 10, 42, 111, 123, 168
sickness 74, 78–79, 85, 112, 113, 146, 152
sin 10, 20, 23, 25, 26, 54, 55, 56, 64–65, 97, 113, 114, 116, 117, 128, 134, 170, 186
sociology 28, 29, 91, 142
speech 128, 136, 151
spiritual direction 29, 113, 116, 122, 163
spirituality 7, 56, 57, 74, 128, 132, 171–172
stress 153
suffering 5, 7, 23, 68, 70, 71, 72, 74, 76, 78, 79, 84, 85, 107, 109, 117, 132, 134, 183, 192
supervision 132, 146, 148, 162–168, 173
support 7, 19, 22, 42, 43, 44, 47, 48, 62, 68, 77, 82, 91, 93, 97, 98, 118, 121, 130, 132, 135, 148, 154, 164–165, 167, 172, 173, 174, 182
symbols 42, 44, 80, 90, 95, 96, 97, 99, 128, 130, 137, 142, 145, 160, 182

theological reflection 28, 63, 64, 84, 110, 164, 166
theology 2, 17, 23, 55, 56, 57, 58, 62, 82, 117, 119, 127

Tillich, Paul 116
time 6, 17, 21–22, 33, 37, 76, 80, 81, 105, 108, 129, 130, 136, 138, 144, 151, 153–154, 166, 172, 173, 178, 179, 181, 187, 188
time off 153, 188
touch 62, 80, 81, 97, 142, 151–152, 168
transcendence 21, 27, 29, 45, 59, 96, 99, 192–193
transference 161
transition 22, 33–48, 60, 63, 75, 93, 96, 97, 98, 99
trauma 40, 46, 47, 68, 73
Trinity 4, 5, 20, 24, 58, 71, 88, 94, 105, 119
Tuckman, Bruce 93

vicarious religion 91, 92, 135
virtue 13, 20, 36, 170
visiting 76, 79, 80, 84, 108, 144, 169, 178, 181, 182
vocation 2, 4, 11, 18, 20, 27, 28, 30, 88, 101, 105, 109, 138, 164, 166, 172, 186, 188, 191
vulnerability 7, 8, 23, 58, 59, 61, 63, 69, 78, 107, 111, 134, 141, 143, 145, 151, 157, 161, 169, 179, 184, 192

Winnicott, Donald 36, 61
wisdom 2, 10, 12, 13, 17, 18, 22, 23, 27–30, 37, 38, 40, 45, 46, 56, 57, 68, 69, 70, 75, 85, 100, 112, 116, 132, 136, 148, 149, 154, 162, 166, 178, 181, 185, 188, 192
worship 3, 30, 58, 67, 87, 90, 91, 92, 93, 95–101, 112, 120, 121, 154, 177
wounded healer 9, 192, 194

youth work 7, 50, 109, 149

www.ingramcontent.com/pod-product-compliance
Lightning Source LLC
Chambersburg PA
CBHW051149290426
44108CB00019B/2657